SPEC Kit 354
Data Curation
May 2017

Cynthia Hudson-Vitale, Washington University in St. Louis Libraries
Heidi Imker, University of Illinois at Urbana-Champaign
Lisa R. Johnston, University of Minnesota Twin Cities Libraries
Jake Carlson, University of Michigan Library
Wendy Kozlowski, Cornell University
Robert Olendorf, Pennsylvania State University
Claire Stewart, University of Minnesota

/ **ASSOCIATION
OF RESEARCH** /
LIBRARIES

SPEC Series Editor: Lee Anne George

Association of Research Libraries
21 Dupont Circle, NW
Suite 800
Washington, DC 20036-1118
T 202.296.2296
F 202.872.0884

ARL.org
pubs@arl.org

ISBN 1-59407-977-3 / 978-1-59407-977-1 print
ISBN 1-59407-978-1 / 978-1-59407-978-8 online

Table of Contents

This page intentionally left blank

Survey Results

Executive Summary

Introduction

Researchers are required by many federal and private funders[1] and publishers[2] to make the digital data underlying their research openly available for sharing and reuse. In order for data to be fully and publicly accessible to search, retrieve, and analyze, specialized curatorial actions should be taken to prepare the data for reuse, including quality assurance, file integrity checks, documentation review, metadata creation for discoverability, file transformations into archival formats, and selection of a suitable license/copyright. Data curation, which may be broadly defined as the active and on-going management of data through its lifecycle of interest and usefulness to scholarly and educational activities[3], is an important role for academic research libraries as we transform our workforce to assume greater digital stewardship responsibilities in the academy.[4-5] Libraries are in the business of identifying, selecting, organizing, describing, preserving, and providing access to information materials, print and digital. And as a cornerstone of the academic institution, libraries are persistent, with a demonstrated and sustainable model for providing services such as collection management, preservation, and access to a broad variety of information. Thus, the care of research data sets is central to our mission.

Although a number of studies and surveys have recently explored data services provided by libraries, they have focused more on the broader concept of research data management (RDM) services, without detailing the policies, staffing, and data curation treatment actions described above. For example, the "E-Science and Data Support Services" report[6] published in 2011 surveyed institutions about staffing and data storage infrastructure broadly. Similarly, research completed by Tenopir et al. in 2011[7] and again in 2015[8] asked library directors at 351 organizations about current and expected infrastructure for research data services. Questions relevant to data curation were broad and touched upon whether support was provided for activities such as metadata creation, the existence of an institutional repository system for data, and deaccessioning of datasets, to name a few. And while generally focused on RDM, the 2013 SPEC survey on research data management services[9] did include a number of questions related to data curation infrastructure and services. These included specific questions about repository technology platforms, total size of datasets, and basic preservation treatment actions, among others. Lee and Stvilia recently highlighted the curation services libraries are providing through local institutional repositories.[10]

Given the rapidly changing technology and data sharing policy ecosystem, curation may not seem scalable to many libraries. In fact, Tenopir et al. found little to no change in data services support among surveyed libraries between 2011 and 2015. Yet, demand for data sharing support has already and will continue to increase given the number of publishers and funders requiring data sharing. The success of sharing and subsequent reuse is predicated on dataset quality, which is difficult to achieve without appropriate curation.

The purpose of this survey was to uncover the current staffing and infrastructure (policy and technical) at ARL member institutions for data curation, understand the current level of demand for data curation services, and discover any challenges that institutions are currently facing regarding providing data curation services. The survey was distributed to the 124 ARL member libraries in January 2017. Eighty (65%) responded by the January 30 deadline.

Current State of Curation Services

The survey results show that a majority of ARL libraries are providing data curation services or that development of these services is underway. Specifically, of the 80 survey respondents, 51 (nearly two thirds) indicated that they are currently providing services to support data curation and another 13 indicated that they are developing these services. Only 20% of the sample, or 16 libraries, indicated that they do not provide nor are actively developing data curation services. Data curation services appear to be a relatively recent initiative; more than half of the libraries that currently provide services (35 of 51) started doing so in 2010 or later.

Looking closer at the 51 institutions that provide data curation services, most (46 or 90%) also provide repository services for data. Twenty-nine have an institutional repository that accepts data. A smaller number (8 or 17%) have a stand-alone data repository. Similar to the responses on data curation services, the majority of these repositories came online in 2010 or later. DSpace is the most common repository platform and is used by 22 of the reporting institutions. Eleven use Dataverse (as either a hosted or a local installation), 10 use Fedora/Hydra, and seven use Islandora. Seventeen respondents use a combination of these or other platforms.

Interest in providing data curation services does not yet appear to have translated into strong staff levels to provide these services. The survey asked how many staff focus 100% of their time and how many spend part of their time on data curation services. The responses show that the majority of libraries place responsibility for data curation services on individuals who have other duties to carry out.

Forty-nine responding libraries reported a total of 293 staff who are involved in data curation activities. Forty-five of these reported they have staff who focus part of their time on data curation (a total of 231 individuals). The number of partial focus staff ranges from one to 15 per library. The percentage of time they spend varies widely by institution, with some reporting 5–10% of time and others indicating it may be as high as 40–50%. (See question 4 for specifics.) Some institutions stated that the amount of staff time spent is variable depending on demand from researchers.

Twenty-eight respondents only have partial focus staff (a total of 143 individuals). Seventeen have both partial focus and exclusive focus staff (88 partial and 39 exclusive). Three libraries have one person who spends all their time on data curation. An outlier reported 20 staff devoted exclusively to these activities.

The 51 responses to a question on the source of demand for data curation services shows it comes from researchers across subject domains. As shown in the graph below, researchers from the life sciences and social sciences are most likely to ask for these services (33 responses each or 65%). Perhaps somewhat surprisingly given the focus STEM disciplines often receive in discussing data, arts & humanities edged out both engineering and applied sciences and the physical sciences (21, 20, and 19 responses respectively). These are followed by other science disciplines.

Figure 1. Demand for data curation services by subject domain

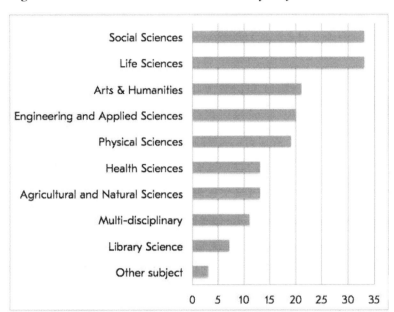

The nascent nature of data curation services and treatments across the ARL institutional landscape is evident in a number of results from this survey. Although the Office of Science and Technology Policy memo on access to federally funded scientific data was released in 2013,[11] library technical and human infrastructure are just now reaching the point of accepting and curating data. Of the 46 libraries that accept data, the majority (26 or 61%) have fewer than 50 data sets in their entire collection. Ten libraries have between 51 and 200 data sets but only seven report having over 200 in their repository. The growth of data deposits seems to be consistent, with 14 libraries receiving approximately one new dataset a month, and three receiving more than 10 a month.

Describing data sets using standard metadata schemas is of significant importance for data discovery, dissemination, and reuse. Yet, there are many schemas to choose from, including general, discipline-specific, and institution specific. Survey respondents indicate six major metadata schemas are in use: DublinCore, MODS, DDI, DataCite, Dataverse (which is based on a number of standards)[12], and MARC. A number of institutions also employ others, such as ISO19115, Geoblacklight, and VRACore4, or custom metadata schemas. Additionally, many organizations use more than one schema for different purposes, and some institutions reported they use up to four.

Many of the data repository services and technologies facilitate both self-deposit and mediated deposit of data (22 of 46 responses or 48%). The majority of data repositories limit the size of file uploads (35 or 78%) with an average reported at around 2.5 GB per file. Thirty-two of the responding libraries (65%) also help researchers prepare their data for deposit to external repositories. As shown in the graph below, the external data repositories they support most often are ICPSR, Figshare, and the Open Science Framework.

Figure 2. External data repositories

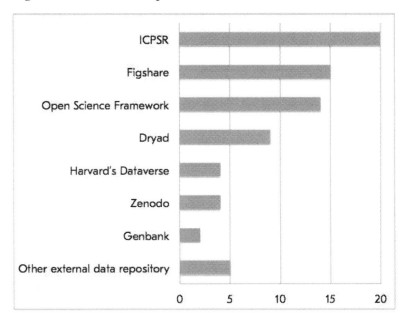

Curation Policies

Curating sensitive data is a topic debated among data repository managers and librarians. Fewer than half of the respondents to a question on private or sensitive data (21 or 42%) reported their service supports sensitive data. One who does explained how the process for curating such data is not insignificant:

> "We collaborated with compliance officers on our campus to establish workflows for sensitive and restricted data, addressing IRB, HIPPA, FERPA, and government and export controlled data. Our service is currently undergoing a formal RQA (research quality assurance) review to ensure regulatory compliance."

While curating sensitive data may not be possible for many institutions, placing embargoes or restricting access by institutional IP is. The majority of respondents (42 of 49 or 86%) report their repository has a feature to allow such restrictions, and some offer embargos that can last for up to 10 years, but their comments indicate it isn't necessarily implemented.

Documentation, such as a readme file, metadata, code books, and methodologies, is an essential component of the research process and often necessary for ensuring the reproducibility of the research. The survey asked which documentation data curation services require from depositors and whether they help depositors create any of it. Of the 45 respondents who answered this question, the majority require and/or help the researcher create metadata. [N.B. Respondents could select both options in their response.] Only 17 institutions require readme files but 32 institutions reported that they provide support in creating them. Only a few respondents require other types of documentation. Overall, it is surprising to learn that while some institutions do not *require* additional documentation, they do *recommend* the inclusion of these types of descriptive information.

Twenty-nine libraries answered a question on which tools and applications they use in their curation treatments. The most commonly used include BagIt (13 responses) and Fixity (12). Bitcurator, FITS, and JHOVE are each used by nine institutions. A few also mentioned DROID and OpenRefine. Half of the respondents use two or more different tools, depending upon their service level.

One tool that many institutions use to ensure access and the citability of research data is a persistent identifier. Many repository platforms and software applications facilitate the creation of persistent identifiers for digital assets, and there are a variety of identifier types available for institutions to adopt. The survey responses indicate that handles are the most commonly employed persistent identifier (26 responses or 59%), followed by DataCite DOI's (25 or 57%), and, to a lesser extent, CrossRef DOI's (9 or 21%), PURLS (5 or 11%), and ARKS (4 or 9%).

Preservation Services

One key component of the data curation lifecycle is data preservation. Preservation services (such as emulation, file audits, migration, secure storage, and succession planning) help ensure that the data and technology is reusable and stable over the long term. Of the 50 respondents to a preservation question, 34 (68%) provide these services for curated data. Fourteen of these indicated they will preserve data for at least 10 years, four others reported between 12 and 25 years, and at least 10 indicated their commitment is to preserve data indefinitely. Others don't specify a time commitment.

The platforms and tools these libraries use for preserving data vary widely, with most respondents selecting "other platform" from the list of answer choices. Those platforms include DSpace, ePrints, LOCKSS, Swift Open Stack, APTrust, and DPN. We suspect this variety is due to the varying degrees of preservation, and the difficulties with pinning down definitions. As one respondent commented, "We presently steer clear of the word preservation, relying instead on long-term stewardship as our nomenclature."

Figure 3. Platforms used for archiving/preservation

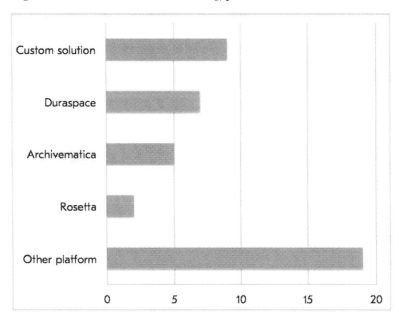

The most common preservation-compliant metadata standards used are MODS and PREMIS (12 of 28 responses each or 43%). There is little standardization across institutions in backup services. Many are employing tape systems and cloud services to ensure redundant copies of the data remain available.

Support for Curation Activities

Data curation services comprise a variety of different types of activities. The survey asked respondents to indicate whether their service provides any of 47 different activities grouped into five different aspects of data curation: ingest, appraisal, processing and review, access, and preservation. If an activity is not currently included as a part of the service, we asked if they plan or aspire to include the activity in the future.

The most universally provided data curation services are ingest activities, which include metadata, deposit agreements, authentication, documentation, file validation, and chain of custody. Forty-five libraries (92%) currently provide one or more of these services and all but chain of custody are offered by more than two-thirds of the libraries. The access category covers 11 activities that are likewise commonly supported. Forty-three libraries currently provide one or more of these services. More than two-thirds provide file download, terms of use, discovery services, embargo, use analytics, metadata brokerage, and data citation. Only 14 provide data visualization, though.

Most of the responding libraries provide some of the 18 processing and review activities. However, this category shows an interesting bimodal distribution of results between activities that are currently supported and those the respondents would like to provide, but are unable to at this time. As one respondent commented:

> "These ten activities are the most difficult to implement because they are the most time consuming and resource intensive. These activities also require a high degree of both technical training and disciplinary knowledge. We are slowly working towards supporting these activities, however some, like peer-review, are and will continue to be out of reach. If depositors/users supply us with this metadata, and/or ask us for assistance, then we will provide this support where possible. However, we cannot currently provide large-scale support across all datasets deposited in our repository."

This bifurcation is also seen for the nine activities in the preservation category and the three appraisal activities.

Figure 4. Support for Ingest Activities

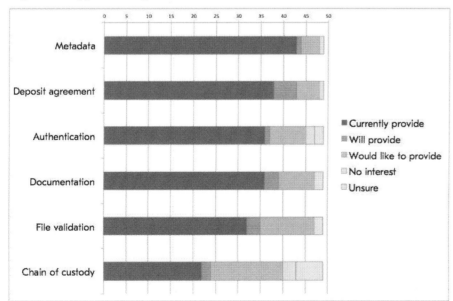

Figure 5. Support for Appraisal Activities

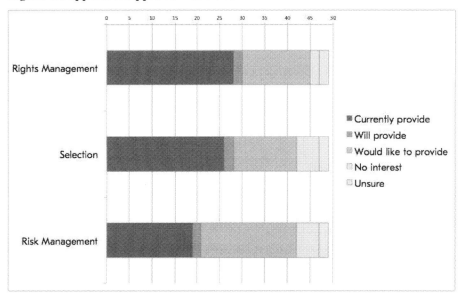

Figure 6. Support for Processing and Review Activities part 1

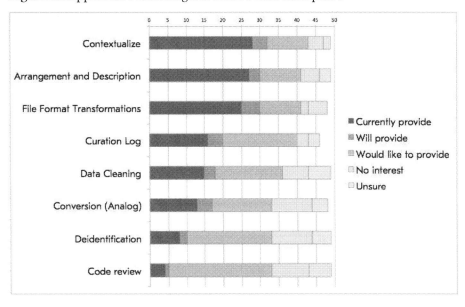

Figure 7. Support for Processing and Review Activities part 2

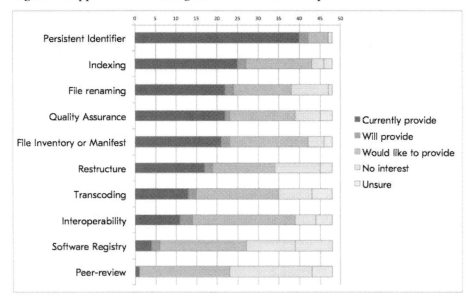

Figure 8. Support for Access Activities

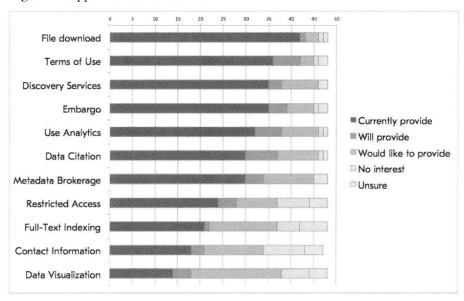

Figure 9. Support for Preservation Activities

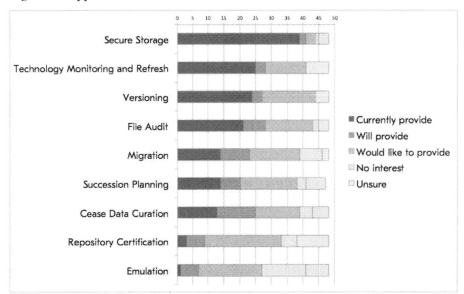

The survey responses indicate many institutions have either already instigated support or are holding steady at their current level of support for a number of curation activities. This holding pattern may be a consequence of resources at hand. The survey data indicate that the more built-in the activity is to the repository platform, the more likely it is to be applied to data. For example, the results show that many institutions are applying handles as PIDs for datasets, which we attribute to convenience because of their widespread presence in IRs. In fact, among the 47 different curation activities scored, assignment of a PID is the activity with the second most universal current support. The activity with the most universal support is, not surprisingly, file download. These curation activities with noticeably uniform levels of support for datasets are frequently a function of the repository technology. Curation activities that are commonly handled by a system, and therefore easier to scale, are more commonly supported than activities that require human intervention. Activities that are not readily supported in current repository systems are more likely to be aspirational. For example, comments on the use of BitCurator explain that while this tool is used in library systems, it is not necessarily applied to data, yet.

Aspirational Curation Activities

Since support for data curation is a relatively new area for libraries, there are quite a few curation activities that librarians would like to perform but are unable to. The table below shows the activities with the largest gap between the number of libraries currently providing it and the number that would like to.

Activity	Currently provide	Plan to or would like to provide	% Difference
Repository Certification	3	30	91%
Code Review	4	29	88%
Emulation	1	26	96%
Peer Review	1	22	96%
Software Registry	4	23	85%
Deidentification	8	25	76%
Interoperability	11	28	72%

Interestingly, there is some disagreement as to the value of providing the data curation activities on this list. In addition to responses indicating a strong interest in these activities, there were also a number of respondents who indicated that they had no interest in providing them or were unsure whether or not they wanted to provide them. The number of respondents who indicated a strong lack of interest or were unsure are listed in the table below.

Activity	No Interest	Unsure	Total % of those providing a response
Repository Certification	5	10	31%
Code Review	10	6	33%
Emulation	14	7	44%
Peer Review	20	5	52%
Software Registry	12	9	44%
Deidentification	11	5	33%
Interoperability	5	4	19%

In both the processing and preservation categories there are a large number of respondents (close to half) who indicated they have no interest in performing these curation activities in the future. The survey results and comments made about data curation activities reflected librarians ambivalence around incorporating them into library services. As one respondent commented, "We believe all this is important, just not things the LIBRARY needs to do or should do."

Peer review appears to be a particularly problematic area for librarians as many respondents appeared to recognize its importance to scholarship, but felt that the complexities of peer review for data put it outside of what libraries can offer. Some of the comments also indicated that while activities such as repository certification and emulation are important, they are not necessary for every library to achieve or to offer. Other comments expressed concern about the ability of libraries to offer these services given limited resources and expertise. Instead, some respondents felt that the data curation activity would be better performed by others, particularly the researcher depositing the data or an IT unit. This schism in the survey responses with some respondents aspiring to provide particular data curation activities and others indicating uncertainty or no interest, is further indication that the library community has not yet come to a shared understanding of the roles they expect to play in providing data curation services.

Challenges

Respondents indicated that they expect to face numerous challenges in providing data curation services in the near future. The survey listed seven aspects of providing these services and all of them were seen as challenging by respondents, receiving an average rating of 3.54 or higher on a 5 point Likert scale (5 = very challenging). The most challenging is having expertise in curating certain domain data. The lowest ranked challenge is changing requirements for data sharing. The comments indicate there is considerable concern about institutional priorities for data curation and funding, increasing demand for services and the library's capacity to scale up to respond to anticipated demand, and the challenges of recruiting and retaining skilled personnel to provide services.

Perceived Importance of Curation Activities

The respondents who reported they are not currently offering data curation services were asked to assign a ranking of importance to each of the 47 possible curation activities listed in the survey, with a rank of "1" meaning that they consider the activity to be essential and a rank of "5" meaning that it is not important. Overall, the activities that received the highest importance rating are in the ingest and access categories.

Providing a persistent identifier was ranked as the most important activity overall (with an average ranking of 1.23). This is followed closely by metadata (1.25), information about terms of use (1.35), allowing file download (1.39), having a deposit agreement from the author (1.5), documentation that describes the data (1.5), a secure storage environment (1.52), a process for rights management (1.54), discovery services for search and retrieval (1.61), and a data citation to enable appropriate attribution by data users (1.65). Many of these highly ranked activities are commonly facilitated through institutional repository platforms and software generally and are not unique to data.

On the other end of the scale, the curation activities that received the lowest rankings of importance are mostly in the processing and review category. They include code review (with an average ranking of 3.04), conversion of data to more usable formats (3.04), data cleaning (3.17), restructuring poorly structured files (3.18), emulation to enable long-term usability of data (3.48), data visualization (3.57), and least important, peer-review (3.91). Many of these lower ranked activities are more specialized to data or are fairly complex in nature. The comments indicated that there are some questions about whether these activities are the responsibility of libraries, the researcher who created the data, or of other units on campus such as central IT. There were also comments questioning whether libraries possess the infrastructure or the expertise needed to carry out these activities. Based on these responses it is not clear that libraries have reached a consensus on a data curation definition and the role of the library in providing research data curation services.

Limitations

Readers of this survey should be aware of its limitations. First, many of the comments indicated that respondents conflated data curation activities with research data management services, and we regret that we did not frame the distinction more explicitly for survey respondents. This indicates that a common understanding of data curation is not widespread or ubiquitous. On the other hand, it also illustrates an opportunity for increased education and outreach to the broader library community.

In a similar vein, many responses concerning library resources and repositories were answered from the context of the greater organization. For instance, several respondents indicated they concurrently use two to four repository platforms for data. However, closer examination of several of the respondents' websites revealed that some of the repositories do not house data or are actually affiliated with other campus units. This may be a result of the survey design, it may suggest that many libraries do not know where their data are going, or that they use several solutions, not all of them owned by their unit, or both.

In many cases, the more quantitative questions, such as the number of FTEs devoted to data curation, made it difficult to determine with precision the amount of effort libraries are expending on data curation activities. Also, when querying the level of support provided by libraries (e.g., currently providing or will provide in the near future, etc.), it appeared that responses were made relative to the library's overall resource pool. In other words, a small institution and a large institution might both have responded at the same level of support, however, in absolute terms there may be a significant difference between the two.

Additionally, analyzing the data and links provided by respondents to related resources indicates that many institutions are providing curation activities only through their institutional repository, and are therefore limited by its technical capabilities. However, other institutions provide additional curation and review of the data files through staff-powered services.

Conclusion

Despite the definitional issues noted above, it is clear from the survey responses that ARL member libraries are increasingly interested in and engaged in providing data curation services. Many of the data curation activities currently performed are those that have been traditionally performed by libraries to support their collections, or are generally offered through an institutional repository. Since many libraries reported curating a relatively small number data sets, it is not surprising to see data curation generally treated as an extension of existing curation services delivered through existing repositories. The survey results suggest that data are treated by many libraries as just another type of content in their collections and do not currently receive specialized treatment or attention, though there are notable exceptions in libraries who have made heavy investments. This may be due, at least in part, to the current low levels of staffing dedicated to performing data curation activities. The high numbers of respondents who indicated that they are planning to or would like to provide additional data curation services implies a strong desire by librarians to invest in this area and improve upon current capabilities.

As we analyzed the numeric data, digested comments, and reviewed representative documents, one major theme that emerged from the survey is the wide variability in data curation services offered. A few institutions reported operation and maintenance of long-standing, established repositories with a high level of sophistication across the majority of curation activities. A larger subset of respondents recently took steps to develop and launch more robust curation services, such as curating data in an established IR or developing a standalone data repository. A final group of survey respondents have established core research data services, namely researcher training, data management plan reviews, and may accept datasets into library collections, but have yet to embark on the larger suite of possible curation activities.

The variability is likely a reflection of the growth, but not yet maturity, of data curation support within libraries. We also found that the associated documentation of services and curation activities varied wildly. All websites naturally look different but the content within further implied a lack of clear definitions for data curation (and associated curation actions) as well as preservation (and associated preservation actions). At this point, the fuzziness is both understandable and perhaps even necessary in order to avoid paralyzing semantic conversations. However, as libraries grow and strengthen their positions as centers of data curation, recursive efforts to convey their activities meaningfully and consistently, both internally and externally, will be of benefit.

In looking to the future, many survey respondents expressed strong concerns about having sufficient support, infrastructure, and staffing to keep up with an anticipated increase in demand for data curation services. Furthermore, the comments made in the survey reveal a polarization among respondents. Some anticipate a need to perform more complex, data-specific activities to support their evolving services. Others are wary of making commitments they may not be able to keep or expressed concern over whether the library is the right agency to perform these activities.

As expectations from funding agencies, publishers, scholarly organizations, and others on data sharing and reuse continue to evolve, libraries expect that the demand for the data curation services will increase. Providing data curation services is a challenging and a resource intensive venture for libraries, but one that has the potential to reframe the role of libraries in providing much needed support for research. By providing a snapshot of the current state of data curation services, staffing, and infrastructure we hope to facilitate interest and discussion about the growth of these services and how libraries can move them forward.

Endnotes

1. See for example the data sharing policy of the National Institutes of Health at https://grants.nih.gov/grants/policy/data_sharing and of the National Science Foundation at https://www.nsf.gov/bfa/dias/policy/dmp.jsp.

2. Some publishers have specific requirements for how authors must publically share the data related to their publication. See the author guidance for data sharing from *PLoS ONE* (http://journals.plos.org/plosone/s/data-availability) or *Nature* (http://www.nature.com/authors/policies/availability.html#data) as examples.

3. University of Illinois Urbana-Champaign School of Information Science. "Specialization in Data Curation." Accessed April 4, 2017. http://www.lis.illinois.edu/academics/programs/specializations/data_curation.

4. DataCure. "Open Letter to PLoS: Libraries' Role in Data Curation," https://datacurepublic.wordpress.com/open-letter-to-plos-libraries-role-in-data-curation/.

5. National Research Council. "Preparing the Workforce for Digital Curation." Washington, DC: National Academies Press, 2015. doi:10.17226/18590.

6. Soehner, Catherine, Catherine Steeves, and Jennifer Ward. "E-Science and Data Support Services: A Study of ARL Member Institutions," August 2010. http://www.arl.org/storage/documents/publications/escience-report-2010.pdf.

7. Tenopir, Carol, Suzie Allard, Kimberly Douglass, Arsev Umur Aydinoglu, Lei Wu, Eleanor Read, Maribeth Manoff, and Mike Frame. "Data Sharing by Scientists: Practices and Perceptions." *PLOS ONE* 6, no. 6 (June 29, 2011): e21101. doi:10.1371/journal.pone.0021101.

8. Tenopir, Carol, Elizabeth D. Dalton, Suzie Allard, Mike Frame, Ivanka Pjesivac, Ben Birch, Danielle Pollock, and Kristina Dorsett. "Changes in Data Sharing and Data Reuse Practices and Perceptions among Scientists Worldwide." *PLOS ONE* 10, no. 8 (August 26, 2015): e0134826. doi:10.1371/journal.pone.0134826.

9. Fearon, Jr., David, Betsy Gunia, Sherry Lake, Barbara E. Pralle, and Andrew L. Sallans. *Research Data Management Services*. SPEC Kit 334. Washington, DC: Association of Research Libraries, July2013. http://publications.arl.org/Research-Data-Management-Services-SPEC-Kit-334/.

10. Lee, Dong Joon, and Besiki Stvilia. "Practices of Research Data Curation in Institutional Repositories: A Qualitative View from Repository Staff." *PLOS ONE* 12, no. 3 (March 16, 2017): e0173987. doi:10.1371/journal.pone.0173987.

11. Office of Science and Technology Policy. "Increasing Access to the Results of Federally Funded Scientific Data." Washington, DC. February 22, 2013. https://obamawhitehouse.archives.gov/sites/default/files/microsites/ostp/ostp_public_access_memo_2013.pdf

12. Castro, Elena. "The Metadata Model of The Dataverse Project: Helping More Data Become Discoverable." IASSIST 2016 Conference, Bergen, Norway. http://dataverse.org/files/dataverseorg/files/iassistposter2016ecastro.pdf

Survey Questions and Responses

This survey was co-designed by **Cynthia Hudson-Vitale**, the Data Services Coordinator in Data and GIS Services at Washington University in St. Louis Libraries and **Heidi Imker**, the director of the Research Data Service at the University of Illinois at Urbana-Champaign in collaboration with the Data Curation Network project team, which also includes (lead) **Lisa R. Johnston**, the Research Data Management/Curation Lead at the University of Minnesota Twin Cities Libraries; **Jake Carlson**, the Research Data Services Manager at the University of Michigan Library; **Wendy Kozlowsk**i, Data Curation Specialist at Cornell University; **Robert Olendorf**, Science Data Librarian at Pennsylvania State University, and **Claire Stewart**, Associate University Librarian for Research and Learning at the University of Minnesota. These results are based on responses from 80 of the 124 ARL member libraries (65%) by the deadline of January 30, 2017. The survey's introductory text and questions are reproduced below, followed by the response data and selected comments from the respondents.

Researchers are required by many federal and private funders and publishers to make the digital data underlying their research openly available for sharing and reuse. Merely making data available, though, is not enough to ensure its on-going viability and re-usability—the data must be curated to ensure/facilitate optimal discovery and re-use.

Data curation may be broadly defined as the active and on-going management of data through its lifecycle of interest and usefulness to scholarly and educational activities. Curatorial actions may include quality assurance, file integrity checks, documentation review, metadata creation for discoverability, file transformations into archival formats, and suitable license/copyright. Data curation services may be provided with or without a local data repository (e.g., allowing deposit of data into the institutional repository or helping local researchers prepare their data for deposit to an external data repository).

Although a number of studies and surveys have recently been published on data services provided by libraries, they have focused more on the broader concept of research data management (RDM) or services, without detailing curation policies, staffing, and treatment actions described above. Although these reports have all been useful, the library community would benefit from a more thorough and comprehensive understanding of needs and services focused specifically on data curation.

The purpose of this survey is to uncover the current infrastructure (policy and technical) at ARL member institutions for data curation, explore the current level of demand for data curation services, and discover any challenges that institutions are currently facing regarding providing these services.

BACKGROUND

1. **Does your institution currently provide research data curation services?** N=80

Yes	51	64%
No	16	20%
In process	13	16%

If you answered "Yes" above, you will be directed to the section "Data Curation Service Demographics."

If you answered "No" or "In process" above, you will be directed to the section "Importance of Data Curation Services."

DATA CURATION SERVICE DEMOGRAPHICS

2. **Please enter the year your institution begin providing data curation services.** N=51

Figure 10. Year data curation services began in five-year groupings

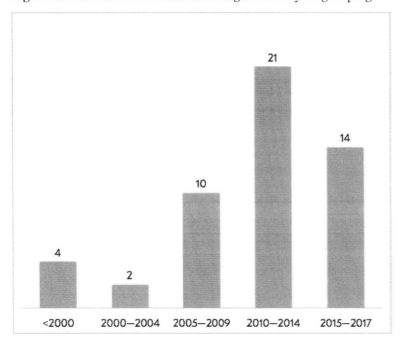

Year	N
1969	1
1977	1
1984	1
1988	1
2000	1
2004	1
2006	3

Year	N
2007	1
2008	3
2009	3
2010	4
2011	4
2012	7
2013	2
2014	4
2015	6
2016	6
2017	2

3. **Who may take advantage of your data curation services?** N=51

Only researchers affiliated with our institution	41	80%
Any researcher regardless of affiliation	10	20%

Comments N=18

Only affiliated researchers N=12

Also researchers who partner with multi-institutional data projects in which our institution participates.

Non-affiliated researchers may deposit materials in CurateND in conjunction with collaborators affiliated with Notre Dame.

Researchers here include faculty and students (such as graduate students) working on projects. These projects are primarily grant funded but don't have to be. We encourage researchers to deposit their data in the appropriate subject repository. If one is not available, then we offer our research data archive.

Researchers with collaborations with Illinois researchers may also contact us.

Some services, such as PURR, are available to Purdue researchers and collaborators whom they invite from other institutions.

The institutional repository (IR) was established in 2004; librarians assist depositors in preparing the metadata for their submissions. Full research data curation services (working with incipient, ongoing, and legacy projects and data) commenced in 2014 with a CLIR/DLF postdoctoral fellow for data curation.

These services were offered exclusively for the Social Science Department until 2012.

This may change provided the outcome of an NSF MRI proposal recently submitted.

Very early stage of providing these services.

We began a formalized data curation program in fall 2016, with the appointment of our data curation librarian. However, we have been providing services on a more informal, ad-hoc basis prior to that, which accounts for some dates prior to 2016 later in the survey.

We include students as well as faculty in "researchers."

We will work with any researcher who contacts us; however, affiliated researchers take precedent and are able to deposit in our data repository. With regard to data curation service provision beginnings, the university has been a leader in digital image and text curation for more than a decade. With regard to digital data, the repository was launched in early 2016.

Any researcher N=6

As a public, land-grant institution, we provide services both to the university and the local community. However, we are willing to provide curation consultations to any researcher, regardless of affiliation, as long as the topic falls within the scope of our expertise.

Primary focus in university-affiliated researchers, however, we will offer support to external researchers.

UBC Dataverse is a service available to researchers affiliated with four universities in British Columbia: Simon Fraser University, University of British Columbia, University of Northern British Columbia, and University of Victoria. Researchers not affiliated with these universities may be granted access to data curation services on a case-by-case basis, but this is rare.

We began curation work with the Sloan Digital Sky Survey in 2006. We have also curated humanities data for at least a decade. Both of these efforts involve researchers from other institutions. We launched our data management services (DMS) group in 2011. The DMS supports JHU researchers only (though they may have collaborators from other institutions as part of their grant proposals). We also have a GIS group that does some data curation activities though not as intensively.

We don't have a specific policy that limits our services to UNM affiliated researchers, and organizationally we have interests in developing state-wide infrastructure and capacity. UNM also has strong institutional linkages with Los Alamos and Sandia National Laboratories and include externally generated content in our institutional repository, which serves both data and document curation roles. We have also worked with multi-institutional programs in integrating their data holdings into our system.

We provide ready access to data curation services but only individuals affiliated with the institution receive free services.

4. **Please indicate how many staff members' work responsibilities focus exclusively (100%) on providing data curation services and how many staff focus partially (less than 100%) on providing data curation services. For staff who focus partially on data curation, please briefly describe about how much time they spend on these services, for example, "2 staff members at 50% time each."** N=50

Exclusively N=49	Partially N=49	Comments N=45
0	1	1 staff member at approx. 80%
0	1	We have no staff who's full time job is to focus on this.
0	1	1 staff member @ 10% time
0	2	We don't allocate a set percentage of time. Librarians who do data curation support spend as much time as necessary responding to researcher requests for assistance.
0	2	2 staff members at < 5% each, depending on need/opportunity
0	2	1 staff member @10% time, 1 staff member @ 2% time
0	2	2 staff as needed.

Exclusively N=49	Partially N=49	Comments N=45
0	2	one at 10%, one at maybe 40%
0	2	1 at 5%, 1 at 20%
0	2	1 at 50%, 1 at 50%
0	3	Total <1FTE
0	3	1 staff member at up to ~5% time, 1 staff member at up to ~15% time, 1 additional staff member (non-library) as needed.
0	3	2 staff at 20%; 1 staff at 10%
0	3	3 staff members are 5–10% each
0	3	3-4 librarians at 5–10% time each
0	5	2 staff members (RDM librarians) at 50%, 3–4 staff members curating a mix of researcher and library content (digital libraries team, GIS developer, research computing lead)
0	5	4 staff members in General Library System: 1 at 50%, 1 at 25%,1 at 10%, 1 at 5%; 1 staff member in DISC: 1 at 25%
0	6	This is very flexible and varied.
0	6	1 at 50%; 1 at 25% (and growing); 3 at 20%; 1 at 10%; plus 3 developers who support the repository infrastructure but don't deal with research data exclusively.
0	7	1%
0	7	7 staff members at about 10% each
0	7	We have a team of 7 librarians who assist with data curation services (training, consultation, etc.) as needed—time commitment varies. For 1 person, it probably amounts to 10% of her time; for the rest, it's probably less than 5% (depending on how you define data curation services).
0	9	1 director of the data repository (30%), 5 data curators at %20 time each, 1 coordinator at 20%, 1 developer as needed (% varies), 1 preservation librarian (10%), and a group of library staff on the research data services team.
0	10	While a program focus area, the work still remains largely project based, therefore ebb and flow—no one reaches >50% averaged across a year.
0	10	6 members of Repository & Data Curation up to 20%, 4 members of Digital Scholarship Services up to 25%
0	11	In the ULS: 2 staff at up to 40% each, additional 6 staff up to 20% each. However in practice time spent is usually below these thresholds and is highly variable. In the Health Sciences Library System: 3 staff up to 50%; in practice highly variable.
0	13	2 staff members have data curation services as at least half of their job (combined 1.3 FTE). 1 staff member maintains repository infrastructure (0.2 FTE). 10 staff members (mostly liaison librarians) provide some level of data curation guidance to researchers (combined 1 FTE). The library's total staff investment in data curation services is estimated to be 2.5 FTE.
0	15	Approximately 15 staff members at approximately 10–15% time each.
1	0	
1	1	50% time (includes data management duties)
1	2	2 staff members at 5–10% time each.

Exclusively N=49	Partially N=49	Comments N=45
1	2	Director of Research Data Services: 65% on data curation services, 35% on other subject librarian, project and administrative duties. Business and Economics Subject Librarian: 10% on data curation issues and tracking with data resources within his area of specialization.
1	4	Four librarians on an "as needed" basis
1	4	This varies, but the 4 staff utilize <25% FTE each.
1	5	Many of the subject librarians help with research data but how much depends on the domain or subject. An estimate would be ~5% for subject librarians and ~25% for the Digital Scholarship librarians. Catalogers just starting ~5–10
1	6	1 staff member at 25%, 2 at 15% and 3 are periodic/episodic.
1	6	1 at 1% time | 1 at 10% time | 1 at 20% time | 3 at % time each
1	7	
1	8	RDS Director, 30%; RDS Data Curation Specialist, 2 × 30%; Repository Services Manager, 10%; Metadata Librarian, 10%; CLIR Postdoc, 10%; Information Design Specialist, 10%; Preservation Librarian, 5%
1	0	
1	0	
2	2	1 staff member at 20%, 1 staff member at 40%
2	9	3 librarians at 80%, 3 librarians at 50%, and 3 librarians at 20%
2	10	This is a part of a significant number of individuals' jobs, but to varying degrees. This includes staff working as liaisons with specific departments, as well as functional specialists whose areas of expertise may impact data curation practice.
4	3	3 staff members at perhaps 20% of their time.
4	12	8 staff 10% or less, 4 staff 50%
7	2	Another faculty librarian is approximately 50% on data; an archivist has 25% commitment to data; Not included are GIS data services (3 FTE); also not including percentage of 33 subject librarians who incorporate data into their regular practice of librarianship (some to a high degree); also not included is a faculty librarian in digital humanities although she deals with data extensively.
8	5	All 5 part-time curation is at 50%.
20	0	

Additional comment N=1

Our Data Coordinating Center has 27 staff supporting the data life cycle, however, I cannot report on the percentage of time they do "curation" services. Additionally, the library has 1 staff member that supports data services.

5. **Which subject domains represent the greatest demand for your data curation services? Check all that apply.** N=51

Life Sciences	33	65%
Social Sciences	33	65%
Arts & Humanities	21	41%
Engineering and Applied Sciences	20	39%

Physical Sciences	19	37%
Agricultural and Natural Sciences	13	26%
Health Sciences	13	26%
Multi-disciplinary	11	22%
Library Science	7	14%
Other subject	3	6%

Please specify the other subject. N=3

Environmental Science

Kellogg Institute for International Studies

New service with very little demand at the moment.

6. **Does your library currently provide local repository services for research data (institutional repository, data repository, other)?** N=51

Yes	46	90%
No	5	10%

LOCAL REPOSITORY SERVICES

7. **Please enter the year your library began providing data repository services.** N=45

Figure 11. Year data repository services began in five-year groupings

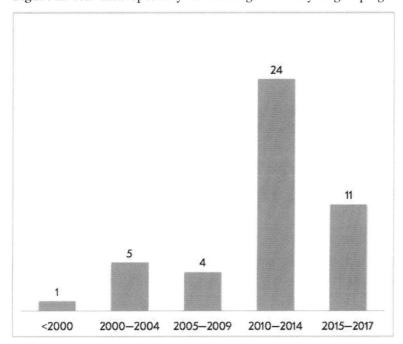

Year	N
1988	1
2002	1
2004	4
2006	1
2009	3
2010	6
2011	3
2012	6
2013	6
2014	3
2015	5
2016	5
2017	1

8. **Which of the following statements best describes your repository service for data?** N=46

An institutional repository that accepts data	29	63%
A stand-alone data repository	8	17%
A disciplinary repository that accepts data	1	2%
Other service	8	17%

Please briefly describe the other service. N=8

A consortial instance of Dataverse local preservation repository.

A constellation of platforms and services that support data curation.

In 2013, UConn Libraries launched the Connecticut Digital Archive, a program that provides long-term preservation services to Connecticut based non-profits. Essentially, UConn Libraries is a customer of itself and uses this technology to support a site that accepts research data.

Our data collection is quite small; we've accepted a couple of deposits for researchers who needed a place to share data, and have also run a small pilot to test expanding the service, something we are still investigating.

Self-deposit institutional repository + 2 format-specific repositories for large collections of images or AV content.

We are currently using a stand-alone data archive but we are migrating to Fedora 4 for both institutional repository and data archive services.

We are mostly reliant on centrally provided services from the California Digital Library. We have an institutional repository that accepts data locally (est. 2010), but are transitioning to the UC-wide DASH stand-alone data sharing repository (est. 2013).

We have several repositories, one for ETDs that technically meets the definition of an IR, but we do not market it as such. We publish a significant disciplinary index and associated repository.

9. **Which of the following platforms are you using for your data repository? Check all that apply.**
N=46

DSpace	22	48%
Fedora/Hydra	10	22%
Islandora	7	15%
Custom solution	7	15%
Dataverse (local installation)	7	15%
Digital Commons/BePress	5	11%
Dataverse (hosted)	4	9%
iRODS	1	2%
Ckan/Dkan	0	—
Other platform	10	22%

Please specify the other platform. N=10

Cuadra Star for the other platform (disciplinary-based), plus, our Islandora instance marries with Fedora Commons.

Dataverse currently provides access to the data but the data are stored and archived within a local system. Once we move to Fedora 4, we will evaluate whether we need to continue using Dataverse, particularly since we are also planning to adopt OSF. We are currently integrating Fedora into OSF.

ePrints

Geoblacklight, OSF for Institutions, ArchiveIT, RStar (homegrown), DataBrary (homegrown)

HUBzero with customized extensions

Islandora/Fedora

Open Science Framework

Rosetta

SobekCM: SobekCM is the software engine which powers the University of Florida Digital Collections (UFDC), Digital Library of the Caribbean (dLOC), and many other digital repositories. SobekCM allows users to discover online resources via semantic and full-text searches, as well as a variety of different browse mechanisms.

We are transitioning now from Islandora to the university's instance of Dataverse. For now, both data and metadata are held in both repositories, but this will change.

If you selected Custom solution above, please briefly describe it. N=7

Hybrid DSpace and Apache platform.

Maria-based, CSS front-end

Our current institutional repository for data is hosted in DSpace. We are in the process of developing a custom Islandora-based solution that will replace DSpace and a BePress instance used for more traditional repository documents.

RStar is our preservation repository, primarily for libraries collections and selected faculty driven products. DataBrary is a video preservation and science platform for the behavioral sciences, developed in partnership with a psychology professor and colleagues group.

Ruby on Rails app that integrates directly with our preservation system.

The local institutional repository is DSpace. The shared system-wide data repository (DASH) is a custom middleware interface that allows researchers to deposit to the CDL Merritt preservation repository.

We host some faculty-created datasets with custom interfaces on virtual machines for specific uses.

10. **How many new data sets does your data repository service receive each month, on average?** N=41

Number of new data sets	N
0	6
<1	11
1	14
2–10	7
>10	3

11. **How many new data sets receive data curation services each month, on average?** N=41

Number of curated data sets	N
0	9
<1	10
1	13
2–10	7
>10	2

Figure 12. Comparison of new data sets received each month and data sets curated each month

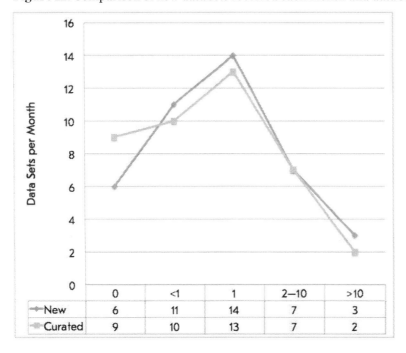

	0	<1	1	2–10	>10
New	6	11	14	7	3
Curated	9	10	13	7	2

12. Please enter the total number of data sets in your repository. N=43

Total number of data sets	N
0	1
1—10	15
11—50	10
51—100	4
101—200	6
>200	7

13. Please enter the total number of data sets that have received curation treatments (reviewed/ enhanced/processed) by library staff. N=43

Total number of curated data sets	N
0	7
1—10	15
11—50	8
51—100	6
101—200	1
>200	3

Figure 13. Comparison of total data sets in the repository and total curated data sets

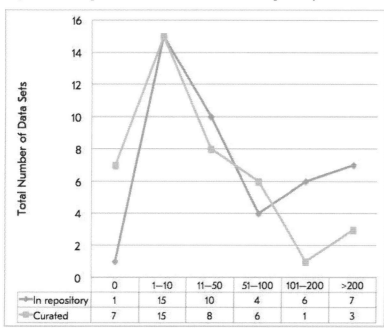

	0	1—10	11—50	51—100	101—200	>200
In repository	1	15	10	4	6	7
Curated	7	15	8	6	1	3

14. What metadata schema are you primarily using for discovery of data? N=43

Dublin Core	30	70%
MODS	9	21%
DDI	8	19%
DataCite	4	9%
Dataverse	3	7%
MARC	1	2%
Other	4	9%

Comments N=43

Citation metadata compiled by Dataverse software.

Consistent with Dataverse 4.0; for general discovery, Dublin Core Terms; DataCite 3.1; Dataverse JSON (for API) used.

DataCite

DD1 — Dataverse; MODS — Islandora

DDI (3 responses)

DDI and Dublin Core (2 responses)

DDI, DC, ISO 19115

Dublin Core (18 responses)

Dublin Core and MODS

Geoblacklight, Dublin Core (modified), MODS, MARC, EAD

Local defined schemas, MODS, VRACore4

METS/MODS; Dublin Core (Zenodo)

Modified Dublin Core (3 responses)

Modified version of DDI and DataCite within ePrints.

MODS (3 responses)

There are different scopes for discovery (structured metadata exposed for harvest, Linked Data, SEO for external search engines such as Google, locally indexed metadata for search and browse, etc.) but the most applicable schemata are qualified Dublin Core and DataCite.

Very basic Dublin Core. Researchers add their own metadata upon deposit. No element is required.

We have a custom developed schema that incorporates elements from other schema but also includes specific elements that emphasize preservation of data. Our DMS consultants work with researchers to fill out a document or template that outlines these metadata elements. Once we move to OSF/Fedora, we will hopefully work with the community to identify a common set of metadata elements that can be incorporated into OSF for more automated procedures.

We use a custom schema somewhat based on DataCite but expressed in MODS.

15. In which of the following ways do researchers deposit data into your data repository? N=46

Both self-deposit and mediated	22	48%
Mediated	14	30%
Self-deposit	10	22%
Other process	0	—

16. Are there individual file size upload limits for your data repository platform? N=45

Yes	35	78%
No	10	22%

If yes, please specify the file size limit. N=35

GB	N
0.1 GB	2
0.2 GB	1
0.5 GB	1
1 GB	1
2 GB	22
5 GB	2
50 GB	1
1000 GB	1

Figure 14. Repository platform data file size upload limits

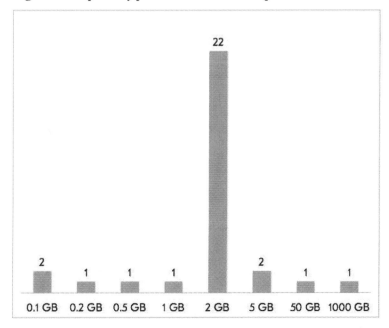

100 MB per file

200 MB

500 MB through self-deposit; mediated deposit doesn't have an explicit limit although we aim to give each researcher 2 TB of space.

1 GB per item

2 GB (17 responses)

2 GB for browser-based uploads, no size limit on the backend

2 GB per file for the self-deposit institutional repository with the option to upload more with assistance from library staff.

2 GB per file per Dataverse policy with option to request more

~5 GB

5 GB unmediated; higher limits mediated

50 GB maximum per file

Dataverse: 2GB; university digital library: no limit

For self deposit we say 2G, in practice it is whatever.

I believe DSpace has a 2 GB limit; we are discussing imposing more stringent limits as we explore expanding services.

No specified limit from Digital Commons, but there is an unspecified practical limit imposed by the HTTP protocol used for file uploads.

Self-deposit: 100 MB | system limit =~ 1TB

Variable

We meet with each researcher to determine the amount of data. Large data sets above 1TB need special consideration.

SUPPORT FOR EXTERNAL REPOSITORIES

17. **Does library staff help researchers prepare or curate their data for deposit to external data repositories outside of your institution?** N=49

Yes	32	65%
No	17	35%

If yes, which external data repositories do you support most often? Check all that apply. N=28

ICPSR	20	71%
Figshare	15	54%
Open Science Framework	14	50%
Dryad	9	32%
Zenodo	4	14%
Harvard's Dataverse	4	14%
Genbank	2	7%
Other external data repository	5	18%

Please specify the other external data repository. N=5

data.cybercommons.org, local EPSCOR project

dbGaP (genomics repository)

journal Dataverse instances

KNB

Open ICPSR

Please enter any additional comments you have about external data repositories. N=21

As mentioned in earlier questions, we have become part of the OSF for institutions (OSF4I) network. We intend to direct our researchers to OSF4I and integrate Fedora into OSF for our data archive. Essentially, researchers will be able to move data between their various storage providers into the JHU Fedora-based archive via OSF4I.

Most of our assistance is informational: how to prepare data management plans, how to locate external data repositories, considerations for naming data files, etc.

Not tracked. Our subject liaisons and research data specialists will advise on the most appropriate repository for a researcher to use whether it is ours or an external repository, e.g., a domain repository. We co-led the development of the re3data.org registry of research data repositories, and one of its use cases is to aid a librarian in helping a patron identify the data repositories that best meet their needs.

Option exists, but has not really happened yet. We recommend general data repositories when the team is cross-institutional, or Dataverse if the team wants to create their own repository.

Support of other external repositories is primarily advocacy and education.

Support provided mostly via DMP preparation consultation.

This is currently an emerging activity area for our team, but we anticipate growing demand in this area.

This is on a case-by-case basis. Help is offered only when the faculty member contacts the library. The service is advertised to the university community but is not a mandatory action. Any request will receive assistance.

We advise researchers about available repositories and help them write data management plans for any repository, but we don't help them write up metadata. We can help them clean and/or organize their data to some extent. Very in-depth projects require grant funding to cover staff time.

We are investigating support for deposit to external data repositories.

We are testing with Zenodo as a general data repository and OSF as a project management of life cycle.

We discourage use of Academia.edu.

We do provide some consultation on external repositories and anticipate doing more in the near future.

We get very few requests for assistance with external data repositories, but we know from reviewing data management plans that our researchers are using external data repositories.

We haven't actually done this yet, but we are game to help!

We often refer researchers to external data repositories given the shortcomings of our existing repository platform. We share general best practices for cleaning and sharing their data regardless of where they plan to upload it.

We receive questions about external repositories and provide general guidance, but we don't offer platform-specific curation services for external repositories.

We would consider doing this but have not been asked.

We would, but no one has asked us to.

We'd be happy to provide this service, but haven't really gotten demand for it.

We're interested in exploring options for researchers who want to use them.

CURATION POLICIES

18. Does your data curation service support private or sensitive data? N=50

Yes	21	42%
No	29	58%

Comments

Answered Yes N=15

Dataverse — yes; Islandora — no

Library will consult on datasets with these characteristics.

Mostly via DMP consultation on how to handle private data.

NARA accessions records exempt from disclosure under the provisions of the Freedom of Information Act, including National Security Classified data.

Not encrypted. Administrators currently have access to all items.

Only in a consultational capacity, and only in selected cases.

Private, yes (we can do embargoes and restrict access), but not sensitive data. The repository does not encrypt data (not HIPAA-compliant).

We collaborated with compliance officers on our campus to establish workflows for sensitive and restricted data, addressing IRB, HIPPA, FERPA, and government and export controlled data. Our service is currently undergoing a formal RQA (research quality assurance) review to ensure regulatory compliance.

We do provide curation support for sensitive data. We just can't publish it.

We provide consultation services on IRB language and have provided data "cleaning" services for some published datasets.

We release the metadata, lock the dataset itself, and provide contact info for accessing the data.

We use Research Vault via our university research computing.

We would be able to provide this support, but have not yet done so.

While our IR does not accept private or sensitive data, we do assist researchers in identifying and depositing data with 3rd part repositories that do support private or sensitive data.

Yes in principle, but we have not handled these requests. We have a protected data network, but have not used it beyond minimal implementation for our IR.

Answered No N=8

In the past (while we were using Islandora as our local repository solution for datasets), we accepted private/sensitive data, but that policy was eschewed due to the move to self-deposit via Dataverse and the inordinate amount of time required for data cleanup.

Not yet, though it is part of our longer-term plans.

Right now, only open projects are being accepted. Cyberinfrastructures are not all equipped to handle sensitive data.

This is subject for a future strategic investigation.

We are currently investigating this for future development.

We check for PII using identity finder.

We require all personal identification information to be removed prior to deposit. We scan embargo data if needed.

We support different levels of access and permissions, but our repositories are not HIPPA compliant.

19. **Does your data curation service support embargoes and/or restricted access conditions?** N=49

Yes   42   86%
No   7   14%

Comments N=17

Answered Yes N=15

Can embargo up to 10 years.

Capacity exists to provide restricted access but we generally support embargos.

Currently the IR is mainly for documents and select, small data sets. Embargoes can be set, but at this time, no data is embargoed.

Dataverse — yes; Islandora — no (We are working on formalizing a collections policy.)

Dataverse allows granular access to data (role-based access restrictions) but does not allow for embargoes.

Embargoes and access conditions are features of a repository, not data curation service support. The "yes" above relates to our depository.

Embargoes, but no other type of restricted access.

Embargos are not available by default but can be enabled if requested. We do not provide restricted access.

Extremely limited—mostly employed when a PID is needed for a publication, and the data need to be withheld until paper is published.

Our service support is geared towards eventual open access conditions, but respects that research processes take time and that researchers may not be initially comfortable making their datasets open. We provide three levels of visibility: Open Access, VT-only, and Restricted.

Some data restricted to research project participants.

Up to 2 years embargo on files (metadata is open) using request a copy feature of DSpace.

When requested.

While we endeavor not to locally archive data with embargoes or restricted access conditions, we work with researchers to find 3rd party repositories that can support complex access protocols.

Yes in principle, but we have not implemented embargoes for research data yet. We have embargoed scholarly publications and ETDs.

Answered No N=2

Not yet, though it is part of our longer-term plans.

This is a subject for a future strategic investigation.

20. **Please indicate if your data curation service** *requires* **any of the following documentation from depositors and if your service** *helps create* **any of the documentation for depositors. Check all that apply.** N=45

Documentation	Requires	Helps create	N
Metadata	33	32	44
Readme files	17	32	37
Code books	3	21	22
Methodology	6	14	18
Scripts or software used to analyze the data	4	13	17
Other documentation	4	12	14
# of respondents	**35**	**40**	**45**

If you selected Requires Other documentation above, please briefly describe what type of documentation. N=4

MODS record

Other documentation includes licensing or permissions.

Rights statements, Gift in Kind form

We require a data description document that describes the content of the files and descriptions of the data elements, software used, etc. for creating and working with the data.

Additional comments N=4

A future service would likely require all (or some) of the above based on the type of data.

Our policy states that all data submissions must contain sufficient documentation to enable reuse.

ReadMe files and Methodology are recommended, not required.

The *repository* requires these. Our data curation services are only tangentially involved in deposit.

If you selected Helps create Other documentation above, please briefly describe what type of documentation. N=10

Basic and custom metadata; reproducibility documentation (with ReproZip); basic codebook definitions OR consult on standards like DDI.

By "help" we mean will advise with one-on-one consultations, provide examples, do review and provide suggestions. We do not ourselves create documentation for researchers.

Curation plans, data management plans, IRB protocol language

Data dictionary

Data management plans for publicly supported research grants

Depending on how the researcher wants to model content, there might be additional information to be added to data sets. This is done on a case-by-case scenario.

MODS record

Rightsstatements.org…very little in the way of CC. GIK form is supplied by university general counsel.

Varies greatly depending on the research project and what is necessary to find, understand, and use the data in the future.

We provide templates for batch upload of metadata and technical language to populate readme files. We will also provide assistance with creating rights statements & licensing.

Additional comments N=3

It is recommended that scientists and researchers include ReadMe files and steps for reproducibility.

Our deposit interface includes a metadata entry form with suggested elements for depositors to fill out.

We use readme.txt templates for many of our data curation activities.

21. **Which of the following tools are you using in your curation treatments and/or activities? Check all that apply.** N=29

BagIt	13	45%
Fixity	12	41%
Bitcurator	9	31%
FITS	9	31%
JHOVE	9	31%
Bulk Extractor	3	10%
Identity Finder	2	7%
Data Accessionner	0	—
Other tool	13	45%

Please briefly describe the other tool. N=13

Currently aware of JHOVE, Bitcurator, and Bulk Extractor. Plan to use in the future.

Currently, there is a custom-built data processor software that we use during ingest. We intend to migrate away from this tool to a community-based tool. We also use a packaging tool developed through the Data Conservancy that creates packages based on a specification that builds on BagIt.

DROID

DROID, mkAIP (locally developed)

Exiftool, MediaInfo

FileAnalyzer

MD5 checksum

NARA uses a variety of tools developed in house and procured to support the content and format verification of born-digital records. These include the Archival Electronic Records Inspection and Control (AERIC) utility for structured data and structured text files.

OpenRefine

OpenRefine, bulkRenameit, xml editor, Fixity is built into the system

PRONOM/DROID, custom python code

The Merritt preservation repository is controlled centrally by CDL. They make use of several tools listed above. CDL created BagIt.

We also have custom import tools we've built.

Comments N=6

Future service offerings likely to include Bitcurator.

Metadata support for research data is through consultation. Our special collection team does use above tools, but not for research data.

Our archives use BitCurator, but we haven't yet used it for data curation work.

The checked items are used in the context of library digitization/digital collection, not for research datasets.

The Dataverse software does the MD5 checksum, on deposit.

We use Bitcurator for content going into Archivematica, but not the repository.

22. **How does your service provide persistent identifiers for data? Check all that apply.** N=44

Handles	26	59%
Datacite DOIs	25	57%
Crossref DOIs	9	21%
PURLs	5	11%
ARKs	4	9%
Other identifier	4	9%

Please specify the other identifier. N=4

Dataverse DOI

EZID to create DOIs; we also support persistent URLs but they're not PURLs or Handles.

We have a URL policy for the university digital library.

We just got Crossref DOIs, so we can issue them but have not done this yet.

Comments N=13

Datasets in Zenodo have DOIs by Zenodo.

DOI's currently offered, but only issued upon request, and point to the Handle URL. Handles are issued for all IR content.

Our hosted Dataverse originally used Handles, but now uses DataCite DOIs.

Our institutional repository provides handles for uploaded items. We have a separate service for researchers interested in minting Datacite DOIs for research purposes.

Previous version of Dataverse created Handles, but the current version generates DataCite DOIs.

Purdue is a founding member of DataCite, and we use and provide DOI service through the EZID platform to other American institutions, professional societies, and other organizations on a cost-recovery basis.

Some of the data was deposited in the IR before we built the data repository. Also, we have a local handle server.

Via EZID service

We are in the process of transitioning to DOIs (currently anticipated to be provided through EZID) with our change over to Digital Commons as our IR moving forward.

We create DataCite DOIs using EZID via Purdue. We also give datasets a unique PURL on our own servers.

We do not have a data repository.

We hope to offer DataCite DOIs soon.

We offer as a service to help mint DOIs but do not necessary host the data. Many research groups have local repositories or methods of presenting the digital asset. There is a MOU as to the importance of working with the library and the maintenance of DOIs minted.

PRESERVATION SERVICES

23. Does your data curation service provide preservation services for data? N=50

Yes	34	68%
No	16	32%

Comments N=16

Answered Yes N=9

A very generalized level of preservation with a commitment to stewarding the content as deposited. Also, instruction around digital preservation issues.

Basic IR (DSpace) includes bit-level preservation and fixity. Items selected for RSTAR include full preservation and assurance of forward migration.

Bit-level preservation and file format transformation and or migration for some files.

I'm not entirely sure what you mean by preservation services. Our approach to date has been focused on preservation in the sense that the data are preservation ready according to our local preservation policy. We have not yet conduced a preservation action (e.g., format migration). It's arguable that in the "precision vs. recall" sense, we have emphasized too much the preservation readiness at the cost of hosting more data (which are less preservation ready).

Ongoing work to standardize across local repository services.

Only as much as provided by the repository platform.

The university digital library does provide preservation. Dataverse is under discussion.

Via the IR

We are currently transitioning from DSpace to LibNOVA for our internal preservation platform, and through our membership in the Digital Preservation Network some data are preserved there as well.

Answered No N=7

Harvard IQSS is responsible for preservation.

Preservation services are not currently offered but will be available when we upgrade to Dataverse 4.6. Archivematica is the platform we expect to use in the future. Backup services are offered.

Solutions are being tested at the moment. More to come.

We are in the process of testing various repository software stacks with the goal of building a Digital Asset IR. Many of the follow up questions on this topic will be part of the process where not only determining the software and cyberinfrastructure but also the policies that are needed to support the IR.

We presently steer clear of the word preservation, relying instead on long-term stewardship as our nomenclature. Users seem to like "archiving" as shorthand, and probably equate that to "preservation." We generate PREMISE metadata and are members of DPN and plan to deposit in 2017. We also leverage LOCKSS, CLOCKSS, and PORTICO for commercially published and government materials.

We provide on-going stewardship for items in our institutional repository, including data. We are moving toward providing digital preservation through DuraCloud and DPN.

We recently created a preservation framework to help shape our approach to this issue. Preservation services are a priority but still in progress. We are a member institution of the Digital Preservation Network.

If yes, please answer the following questions.

If no, please continue to the next screen.

24. **Please enter the number of years your service will preserve the curated data.** N=35

Number of years	N
5	5
5+	3
7	2
10	4
12	1
20	2
25	1
Indefinitely	10

Comments N=24

Aiming for perpetual access.

At least 10 years

Currently, we preserve indefinitely.

Five is mandated by the university, our policy goes up to seven, but we are willing to preserve indefinitely, as well as follow the policies prescribed by granting agencies.

It's free for <1 TB "indefinitely." Above 1 TB, we have a separate price structure for 5-year preservation vs. indefinite preservation per TB.

NARA preserves its accessioned holdings "for the life of the republic."

Originally data in the repository was scheduled to be preserved indefinitely. However, that has been revised to the "useful life of the data."

Our internal preservation policy/system assures 10 years of preservation before assessment for continued archiving. The content that we place into the Digital Preservation Network is assured a 20+ year preservation life.

Preserved indefinitely.

PURR is a university core research facility that is jointly managed by the library, IT, and research office with a budget and commitment to maintaining access to data for a minimum of 10 years. At the end of 10 years, data are remanded to the library and managed under its collection development policies and practices. The library has a policy and framework for making selection decisions at the end of this initial commitment with the intention of treating data as we treat our other unique collections, which is to say, preservation and access much longer into the future beyond the initial 10 years.

The current policy is to preserve the data for five years past the life of a grant. If preservation action is necessary during this time frame, we would conduct it.

"The repository guarantees archival and long-term access" but no specific retention schedule is provided.

This is a difficult question since right now all documents are thought to be "forever" but those digital assets (datasets) have not had a policy defined as to how long.

This is not a defined term, rather, it is subject to the library's own collection policy and/or specific requirements of the funding/program for which the data were created.

Varies.

We are re-visiting this policy [indefinitely].

We commit to 10 years and then a review. However, we anticipate holding the data for much longer.

We commit to preserve some curated data as long as possible. Our preservation policy outlines specific levels of commitment.

We do not currently specify the number of years.

We make no specific time commitment, but use the phrase "committed to preserving the binary form of the digital object."

We promise a minimum of five years, no matter the state of the dataset.

We will keep the data until the research requests it removal.

We've implemented a retention period of five years. This means that at the end of five years after deposit the data will be reviewed and a determination will be made to continue to preserve or remove data. This decision is made in cooperation with the researcher(s).

Will preserve longer [than 20 years] if funding allows.

25. **Which of the following platforms are you using for your archiving/preservation solution/ management? Check all that apply.** N=34

Custom solution	9	27%
Duraspace	7	21%
Archivematica	5	15%
Rosetta	2	6%
Preservica	0	—
Other platform	19	56%

Please specify the other platform. N=18

APTrust

Archivespace, other solutions

Consortial custom preservation pipeline is under construction using Archivematica, Globus Publication, and customized code. Files will originate at individual Canadian repositories, proceed through the pipeline, with preservation copies held at ComputeCanada.

DAITSS (Dark Archive in the Sunshine State) coordinated by the statewide consortium, FALSC.

Dataverse

DPN

DSpace

DSpace, LibNOVA, Digital Preservation Network (Duraspace serves as an ingest point into DPN)

Fedora

Hydra Fedora

Just the base ePrints IR platform

LOCKSS enabled at host Dataverse instance.

MetaArchive, which provides governance and organizational sustainability in addition to a LOCKSS network that maintains fixity and seven geographically dispersed copies of our archived datasets.

NARA uses the Electronic Records Archives (ERA) to preserve its archival electronic records holdings.

Our Fedora repository provides preservation of all data objects.

Swift Open Stack

We have the Fedora/Islandora, which has preservation features such as fixity, checksums. We also have a disaster recovery solution.

Work underway now to redesign hydra applications preservation services and integrating Archivematica into preservation workflow.

26. **What metadata schema are you using for the preservation of data? Check all that apply.** N=28

MODS	12	43%
PREMIS	12	43%
METS	10	36%
Other schema	10	36%

Please specify the other schema. N=10

Dublin Core

Dublin Core. We are not using PREMIS to record preservation events at the moment. It is a goal.

FOXML

NARA uses the Electronic Records Archives (ERA) to preserve its archival electronic records holdings. ERA has a metadata schema known as the ACE.

None

Not sure

Not sure which schema is used by host Dataverse.

Rosetta DNX, based on PREMIS

We also use FGDC and can accommodate specific standards if the loss of information is too great with the mapping to MODS.

Work underway to standardize.

27. **How are you backing up the data sets currently curated? Check all that apply.** N=35

Cloud Services (AWS, DropBox, Box, Duraspace, etc.)	10	29%
DPN	6	17%
Local LOCKSS	2	6%
CLOCKSS	0	—
Portico	0	—
Other service	24	69%

Please briefly describe the other service. N=22

APTrust

British Columbia cloud service (EduCloud)

Campus IT

Currently, an ISILON storage system, duplicated across two locations, with a 3rd tape backup offsite. Looking into integration with AWS.

Custom blend of onsite and offsite storage, including services from Comvault, datasafe, and Iron Mountain.

Data-PASS partners per Dataverse

In addition to MetaArchive, we utilize RAID, UPS, temperature-monitoring software, anti-virus, and auditing and hardening software, as well as multiple layers of backup: Bacula for daily incremental, weekly differential, and monthly full local backups; Dirvish for daily snapshots that are stored in a different data center; and twice-yearly full system dumps to tape using Symantec NetBackup. This is documented internally in our disaster recovery plan.

IRODS to manage replication and backup with three copies of each file, including one tape storage.

Local and remote disk-to-disk back up.

Local curated data (e.g., DSpace) are backed up through the campus IT backup service. Some content is also locally backed up onto RAID configured external hard drives.

Local tape archive, consortial storage cloud (OLRC)

LOCKSS enabled at host Dataverse instance.

Multiple data centres

NARA uses the Electronic Records Archives (ERA) to preserve its archival electronic records holdings. Backups are made to LTO tape.

Off-site tape mirror and AP Trust

Offsite LTOT backup system

Snapshots and we use a tool (I forgot the name). We are also looking into cloud services.

Tape backup with remote duplication and DAITSS.

Tape!

Triple offsite backups to tape

Two local copies in different buildings on campus and a third copy in Amazon Glacier.

We are currently using local storage/backup with offsite copies. But we are evaluating third party possibilities including those mentioned on this list (and also APTrust).

SUPPORT FOR INGEST ACTIVITIES

Here are descriptions of six data curation ingest activities.

Authentication: The process of confirming the identity of a person, generally the depositor, who is contributing data to the data repository. (e.g., password authentication or authorization via digital signature). Used for tracking provenance of the data files.

Chain of Custody: Intentional recording of provenance metadata of the files (e.g., metadata about who created the file, when it was last edited, etc.) in order to preserve file authenticity when data are transferred to third parties.

Deposit Agreement: The certification by the data author (or depositor) that the data conform to all policies and conditions (e.g., do not violate any legal restrictions placed on the data) and are fit for deposit into the repository. A deposit agreement may also include rights transfer to the repository for ongoing stewardship.

Documentation: Information describing any necessary information to use and understand the data. Documentation may be structured (e.g., a code book) or unstructured (e.g., a plain text "Readme" file).

File Validation: A computational process to ensure that the intended data transfer to a repository was perfect and complete using means such as generating and validating file checksums (e.g., test if a digital file has changed at the bit level) and format validation to ensure that file types match their extensions.

Metadata: Information about a data set that is structured (often in machine-readable format) for purposes of search and retrieval. Metadata elements may include basic information (e.g. title, author, date created, etc.) and/or specific elements inherent to datasets (e.g., spatial coverage, time periods).

28. **Please indicate your institution's level of support for these data curation ingest activities on a scale of 1 to 5 where 1=currently providing; 2=will provide in the near future; 3=would like to provide, but unable to at this time; 4=no interest/desire to provide; 5=unsure.** N=49

Activity	1	2	3	4	5
Metadata	43	1	4	0	1
Deposit agreement	38	5	5	1	0
Authentication	36	1	8	2	2
Documentation	36	3	8	0	2
File validation	32	3	12	0	2
Chain of custody	22	2	16	3	6
# of respondents	45	9	22	5	9

Comments N=10

Authentication and chain of custody are not done at the level described here, in part because we allow for unmediated ingest. We are using ORCID to login to Zenodo to ingest data from a GitHub account by linking to the UFID/Gatorlink authentication.

Deposit agreements have been done on an ad hoc basis. Formal agreement currently making it's way through legal for approval.

For file validation and chain of custody, we are using whatever is provided by Bepress during file upload.

IR is currently undergoing policy changes that affect this area.

Like many groups, the infrastructure and work was quickly rushed to production while not all the services, policies and procedures, and distribution of tasks have been fully formed and vetted.

RE Chain of custody: we do this currently, but it's not consistent enough for me to say it's rigorous enough to provide a true record of provenance.

Self-deposit IR supports these activities.

These levels have changed over time but the ratings reflect our current situation.

This is a mediated process that allows us to ensure authentication, chain of custody, and metadata. We are working to provide better file validation.

We provide support but some elements (metadata, documentation) are not as robust as they could be given that our repository is self-service.

SUPPORT FOR APPRAISAL ACTIVITIES

Here are descriptions of three data curation appraisal activities.

Rights Management: The process of tracking and managing ownership and copyright inherent to a data set as well as monitoring conditions and policies for access and reuse (e.g., licenses and data use agreements).

Risk Management: The process of reviewing data for known risks such as confidentiality issues inherent to human subjects data, sensitive information (e.g., sexual histories, credit card information) or data regulated by law (e.g. HIPAA, FERPA) and taking actions to reject or facilitate remediation (e.g., de-identification services) when necessary.

Selection: The result of a successful appraisal. The data are determined appropriate for acceptance and ingest into the repository according to local collection policy and practice.

29. **Please indicate your institution's level of support for these data curation appraisal activities on a scale of 1 to 5 where 1=currently providing; 2=will provide in the near future; 3=would like to provide, but unable to at this time; 4=no interest/desire to provide; 5=unsure.** N=49

Activity	1	2	3	4	5
Rights Management	28	2	15	2	2
Selection	26	2	14	5	2
Risk Management	19	2	21	5	2
# of respondents	34	4	23	9	4

Comments N=13

Currently, "risk management" responsibility is placed on the submitter. Moderated submissions are evaluated by the curator, but self-submitted datasets are not.

For selection, all data submissions undergo a review before acceptance.

Initial plan is to make researchers responsible for certifying no sensitive information is in the dataset and that there are no copyright issues.

RE Risk Management: we provide guidance and conduct preliminary checks but depositors are ultimately responsible. RE Selection: policies are currently under review.

Saying we currently provide these services is a bit of a misnomer. Our data is self-deposited. Researchers do a click through acknowledgment that they have the rights to make the data available and there is no risky/sensitive data included. Appraisal is simple. Our policy is that if a researcher wants to deposit, they can—as long as they click through the rights and licensing terms.

We advise depositors/users on these issues as requested; however, we do not review incoming datasets unless flagged by curation staff or asked by the depositor/user.

We confirm (verbally or in writing) the right of the depositor to deposit content into the archive (either for dark archival storage or open access). If ownership/copyright monitoring is not integrated into the archival platform, it is not manually tracked.

We do not have intensive appraisal practices. If it is research data from the university community with adequate documentation, we will accept it. We ask about copyright and licensing, but we do not assess datasets.

We do not review each data set for risk on deposit. Our Dataverse is self-deposit. We rely on the researcher to comply with stated deposit agreement.

We have ongoing working groups around rights management and a review program in place for risk management. As it is a self-deposit model, we have no interest in pre-appraisal, though we do work with researchers to make their data suitable for deposit.

We have to do this as our repository cannot accept at this time data sets that have PII.

We may be moving away from providing selection appraisal, to a more open self-deposit model. We will be selective about the audience to which we provide a high level of curation service (e.g., more for faculty, less for students).

We use an unmediated ingest process; however, our data sources are mandated to follow university privacy policies distinguishing between restricted data (uses ResearchVault for secure storage) and sensitive data (uses Gatorbox for encrypted storage).

SUPPORT FOR PROCESSING AND REVIEW ACTIVITIES PART 1

Here are descriptions of eight data curation processing and review activities.

Arrangement and Description: The re-organization of files (e.g., new folder directory structure) in a dataset that may also involve the creation of new file names, file descriptions, and the recording of technical metadata inherent to the files (e.g., date last modified).

Code Review: Run and validate computer code (e.g., look for missing files and/or errors) in order to find mistakes overlooked in the initial development phase, improving the overall quality of software.

Contextualize: Use metadata to link the data set to related publications, dissertations, and/or projects that provide added context to how the data were generated and why.

Conversion (Analog): In effort to increase the usability of a data set, the information is transferred into digital file formats (e.g., analog data keyed into a database). Note: digital conversion is also used to convert "fixed" data (e.g., PDF formats) into machine-readable formats.

Curation Log: A written record of any changes made to the data during the curation process and by whom. File is often preserved as part of the overall record.

Data Cleaning: A process used to improve data quality by detecting and correcting (or removing) defects & errors in data.

Deidentification: Redacting or removing personally identifiable or protected information (e.g., sensitive geographic locations) from a dataset prior to sharing with third parties.

File Format Transformations: Transform files into open, non-proprietary file formats that broaden the potential for long-term reuse and ensure that additional preservation actions might be taken in the future. Note: Retention of the original file formats may be necessary if data transfer is not perfect.

30. **Please indicate your institution's level of support for these data curation processing and review activities on a scale of 1 to 5 where 1=currently providing; 2=will provide in the near future; 3=would like to provide, but unable to at this time; 4=no interest/desire to provide; 5=unsure. N=49**

Activity	1	2	3	4	5
Contextualize	28	4	11	4	2
Arrangement and Description	27	3	11	5	3
File Format Transformations	25	5	11	2	5
Curation Log	16	4	20	3	3
Data Cleaning	15	3	18	7	6
Conversion (Analog)	13	4	16	11	4
Deidentification	8	2	23	11	5
Code review	4	1	28	10	6
# of respondents	**38**	**10**	**41**	**22**	**10**

Comments N=15

Code review is on a case-by-case basis if we have the expertise. Conversion from analog comes up with archival material or lab notebooks, we scan but so far do not convert to machine-actionable, Deidentification is something we want to do but need partners on campus.

Dataverse automatically converts well-formed Excel spreadsheets to .csv.

For deidentification, it's unlikely we will perform the service directly given potential legal, compliance, etc. issues. We do provide training for both data managers and researchers about best practices and possible tools for deidentification.

For file format transformations, we can handle only the basic, as in MS Office formats to open formats. We cannot handle at this time formats such as R or that are from specific machines and must use those machines to run the code.

In some instances, we do undertake making corrections to the data, however, the quality of the data remains the responsibility of the depositor.

Most of the above is particularly for libraries collections.

Most of these services are provided ad-hoc. We will provide them when requested, however, we do not yet have an established service for data sets. Additionally, our Data Coordinating Center provides a lot of these services on the medical campus.

Multiple internal studies are currently underway looking at support for these data curation issues.

Note that some of these services are provided as needed and are not necessarily automated or integrated into a system.

Reluctantly toggled for "code review": we've done related HTML review for "research-based websites" that we've acquired, cleaned/modified, and otherwise curated.

Some conversion may occur through our digital collections unit if the collection is unique; however, this is more common for cultural heritage materials than research datasets.

Some of these processes are supported by training, but not performed by library staff.

Staff limitations contribute to the "3" responses above.

There can be significant costs associated with the reprocessing of information. At this time, that is not a cost the libraries are willing to accept. However, that does not mean that as new formats are adopted that there would be an associated method that would be made available for the individual wanting the data could use as a roadmap.

We might do some of these things if our library selects a dataset to preserve forever (Nobel Prize winner's lab notebooks), or if a researcher provided grant funding for library staff involvement.

SUPPORT FOR PROCESSING AND REVIEW ACTIVITIES PART 2

Here are descriptions of ten more data curation processing and review activities.

File Inventory or Manifest: The data files are inspected periodically and the number, file types (extensions), and file sizes of the data are understood and documented. Any missing, duplicate, or corrupt (e.g., unable to open) files are discovered.

File Renaming: To rename files in a dataset, often to standardize and/or reflect important metadata.

Indexing: Verify all metadata provided by the author and crosswalk to descriptive and administrative metadata compliant with a standard format for repository interoperability.

Interoperability: Formatting the data using a disciplinary standard for better integration with other datasets and/or systems.

Peer-review: The review of a data set by an expert with similar credentials and subject knowledge as the data creator for the purposes of validating the soundness and trustworthiness of the file contents.

Persistent Identifier: A URL (or Uniform Resource Locator) that is monitored by an authority to ensure a stable web location for consistent citation and long-term discoverability. Provides redirection when necessary (e.g., a Digital Object Identifier or DOI).

Quality Assurance: Ensure that all documentation and metadata are comprehensive and complete. Example actions might include: open and run the data files; inspect the contents in order to validate, clean, and/or enhance data for future use; look for missing documentation about codes used, the significance of "null" and "blank" values, or unclear acronyms.

Restructure: Organize and/or reformat poorly structured data files to clarify their meaning and importance.

Software Registry: Maintain copies of modern and obsolete versions of software (and any relevant code libraries) so that data may be opened/used overtime.

Transcoding: With audio and video files, detect technical metadata (min resolution, audio/video codec) and encode files in ways that optimize reuse and long-term preservation actions (e.g., Convert QuickTime files to MPEG4).

31. **Please indicate your institution's level of support for these data curation processing and review activities on a scale of 1 to 5 where 1=currently providing; 2=will provide in the near future; 3=would like to provide, but unable to at this time; 4=no interest/desire to provide; 5=unsure.** N=48

Activity	1	2	3	4	5
Persistent Identifier	40	2	5	0	1
Indexing	25	2	16	3	2
File renaming	22	2	14	9	1
Quality Assurance	22	1	16	6	3
File Inventory or Manifest	21	2	19	4	2
Restructure	17	2	15	11	3
Transcoding	13	2	20	8	5
Interoperability	11	3	25	5	4
Software Registry	4	2	21	12	9
Peer-review	1	0	22	20	5
# of respondents	42	9	40	25	15

Comments N=9

For some of these activities, we already support some, but not all, aspects described herein (e.g., we verify metadata but don't crosswalk, we ensure documentation are comprehensive and complete, but we don't open and run data files). We have not yet received AV materials as part of our data management programs.

For those marked 1, we do a pretty minimal amount, e.g., might do file renaming or restructuring, or metadata for a group or set of files, but not for each individual file.

Most of the above is for libraries collections.

Peer-review: Dataverse provides support for anonymous review of data sets. Transcoding is done as needed by a unit outside of Data Curation.

Some of these activities (file renaming, restructure) happen at initial ingest but there is no periodic review.

Some of these are supported via training, not directly by work performed by library staff.

Studies are currently underway to address these data curation issues.

These ten activities are the most difficult to implement because they are the most time consuming and resource intensive. These activities also require a high degree of both technical training and disciplinary knowledge. We are slowly working towards supporting these activities, however, some, like peer-review, are and will continue to be out of reach. If depositors/users supply us with this metadata, and/or ask us for assistance, then we will provide this support where possible. However, we cannot currently provide large-scale support across all datasets deposited in our repository.

We archive software locally only if it is provided with the data by the researcher. We do, however, use DROID to identify file formats and record the PUID in order to use the PRONOM registry to monitor and mitigate software and format obsolescence. If you consider this approach to fit the criteria of a software registry, I would change this line from 'unsure' to 'currently providing'.

SUPPORT FOR ACCESS ACTIVITIES

Here are descriptions of eleven data curation access activities.

Contact Information: Keep up-to-date contact information for the data authors and/or the contact persons in order to facilitate connection with third-party users. Often involves managing ephemeral information that will change over time.

Data Citation: Display of a recommended bibliographic citation for a dataset to enable appropriate attribution by third-party users in order to formally incorporate data reuse as part of the scholarly ecosystem.

Data Visualization: The presentation of pictorial and/or graphical representations of a data set used to identify patterns, detect errors, and/or demonstrate the extent of a data set to third party users.

Discovery Services: Services that incorporate machine-based search and retrieval functionality that help users identify what data exist, where the data are located, and how can they be accessed (e.g., full-text indexing or web optimization).

Embargo: To restrict or mediate access to a data set, usually for a set period of time. In some cases an embargo may be used to protect not only access, but any knowledge that the data exist.

File Download: Allow access to the data materials by authorized third parties.

Full-Text Indexing: Enhance the data for discovery purposes by generating search-engine-optimized formats of the text inherent to the data.

Metadata Brokerage: Active dissemination of a data set's metadata to search and discovery services (e.g., article databases, catalogs, web-based indexes) for federated search and discovery.

Restricted Access: In order to maintain the privacy of research subjects without losing integral components of the data, some data access will be protected and/or mediated to individuals that meet predefined criteria.

Terms of Use: Information provided to end users of a data set that outline the requirements or conditions for use (e.g., a Creative Commons License).

Use Analytics: Monitor and record how often data are viewed, requested, and/or downloaded. Track and report reuse metrics, such as data citations and impact measures for the data over time.

32. **Please indicate your institution's level of support for these data curation access activities on a scale of 1 to 5 where 1=currently providing; 2=will provide in the near future; 3=would like to provide, but unable to at this time; 4=no interest/desire to provide; 5=unsure. N=48**

Activity	1	2	3	4	5
File download	42	1	3	1	1
Terms of Use	36	6	3	1	2
Discovery Services	35	3	8	0	2
Embargo	35	4	6	1	2
Use Analytics	32	6	8	1	1
Data Citation	30	7	9	1	1
Metadata Brokerage	30	4	11	0	3
Restricted Access	24	4	9	7	4
Full-Text Indexing	21	1	15	5	6
Contact Information	18	3	13	9	4
Data Visualization	14	4	20	6	4
# of respondents	43	17	35	18	13

Comments N=10

Current platform analytics has limited capability and functionality at this time.

For Contact Information, we require this from depositors and verify it upon deposit, but we do not go back and check that it is still valid at a later date.

Full-text indexing is available on PDF files and any metadata only.

Most of the above is for libraries collections.

Terms of use are in review by the university counsel's office.

Terms of use provided when known and specified by the depositor.

Use analytics only include data viewed and download totals.

We are a part of SHARE.

We are currently reviewing and revising our terms and conditions with the goal of simplifying them and perhaps converging on a Creative Commons license instead.

We require one author to be designated as the corresponding author for each dataset, however, we have no ability to update this information if the person leaves the university or otherwise declines to update their contact information in the repository. We provide limited full-text indexing with various approaches for enhancing how the content of datasets can be leveraged to improve findability, thumbnails, snippets, etc.

SUPPORT FOR PRESERVATION ACTIVITIES

Here are descriptions of nine data curation preservation activities.

Cease Data Curation: Plan for any contingencies that will ultimately terminate access to the data. For example, providing tombstones or metadata records for data that have been deselected and removed from stewardship.

Emulation: Provide legacy system configurations in modern equipment in order to ensure long-term usability of data (e.g., arcade games emulated on modern web-browsers)

File Audit: Periodic review of the digital integrity of the data files and taking action when needed to protect data from digital erosion (e.g., bitrot) and/or hardware failure.

Migration: Monitor and anticipate file format obsolescence and, as needed, transform obsolete file formats to new formats as standards and use dictate.

Repository Certification: The technical and administrative capacities of the repository undergo review through a transparent and well-documented process by a trusted third-party accreditation body (e.g., TRAC, or Data Seal of Approval).

Secure Storage: Data files are properly stored in a well-configured (in terms of hardware and software) storage environment that is routinely backed-up and physically protected. Perform routine fixity checks (to detect degradation or loss) and provide recovery services as needed.

Succession Planning: Planning for contingency, and/or escrow arrangements, in the case that the repository (or other entity responsible) ceases to operate or the institution substantially changes its scope.

Technology Monitoring and Refresh: Formal, periodic review and assessment to ensure responsiveness to technological developments and evolving requirements of the digital infrastructure and hardware storing the data.

Versioning: Provide mechanisms to ingest new versions of the data overtime that includes metadata describing the version history and any changes made for each version.

33. **Please indicate your institution's level of support for these data curation preservation activities on a scale of 1 to 5 where 1=currently providing; 2=will provide in the near future; 3=would like to provide, but unable to at this time; 4=no interest/desire to provide; 5=unsure.** N=48

Activity	1	2	3	4	5
Secure Storage	39	2	3	1	3
Technology Monitoring and Refresh	25	3	13	0	7
Versioning	24	3	17	0	4
File Audit	21	7	15	2	3
Migration	14	9	16	7	2
Succession Planning	14	6	18	3	6
Cease Data Curation	13	12	14	4	5
Repository Certification	3	6	24	5	10
Emulation	1	6	20	14	7
# of respondents	39	28	39	21	18

Comments N=7

All preservation activities take place at the host Dataverse instance.

Archivematica will provide these features and is part of planned future development.

HUBzero has the capability to provide emulation and to wrap and make software applications available to be executed over the web, much like a terminal server. Ideally, we would like to leverage this capability to make executable tools available with data and to enable online workflow execution and reproducibility, but to date we have only published a linux desktop as a proof-of-concept.

Some items are either taken care of at the consortial level or are subject to consortial prioritizing.

Some of these activities are dependent on infrastructures provided by departments outside the Libraries but within the university.

Succession planning documentation is pending review.

We have the capacity for versioning but it isn't implemented as an automatic function at this time.

CHALLENGES

34. Please indicate how challenging you expect the following aspects of data curation to be in the next 3 to 5 years on a scale of 1 to 5 where 1=Not challenging and 5=Very challenging. N=50

Aspects of Data Curation	1	2	3	4	5	Rating Average
Expertise in curating certain domain data	1	2	11	17	19	4.02
Scaling curation services with increased demand	1	5	11	14	19	3.90
Training and retooling library staff to support data curation services	2	4	14	14	16	3.76
Outreach/Marketing of services	1	9	10	19	11	3.60
Recruiting and retaining data curation staff	3	9	10	13	15	3.56
Keeping up with technology changes	2	6	15	16	11	3.56
Changing journal/funder/domain requirements for data sharing	1	8	16	13	12	3.54
# of respondents	6	24	40	41	37	

Note: A higher average rating indicates a more challenging aspect.

35. Please enter any additional comments you have about data curation challenges. N=16

All dependent on institutional priorities.

Being able to hire IT to ensure infrastructure is stable and can be developed over time.

Demand still relatively low.

Developing successful use cases will aid in funding, infrastructure, and resources support. ROI is crucial.

Each new dataset seems to be unique among all previously accepted data.

In many of these cases, these aspects of data curation have already begun, but I imagine that this will be an ongoing process.

Perception of services will be a big issue; as data curation becomes "popular." It will still get conflated with storage or at least ease of storage, so demand could rise steeply.

RE scaling to meet increased demand: I'd like to be more optimistic and say we'll be getting enough datasets that this will be a challenge over the next 3–5 years, but I've thought that for the last 3–5 years also and we've not seen a large enough increase to prevent us from offering these services.

Recruiting is not so hard, but retaining is.

Scaling is and will be the biggest challenge for us.

So far demand has not been a limiting factor.

Some of these issues were more challenging when we began but have since become much easier as we've become more established. The two biggest challenges remain raising awareness of data curation needs and helping our research community understand that the library offers services to help them. Another big challenge is recruiting and retaining staff. We've had three principal research data employees recruited by other institutions in the last two years, and one position was in search and screen for 25 months until we were able to fill it.

The funding models in the current budget constraints that universities are in for the foreseeable future make it hard. Training and marketing are easy, but long-term commitments are harder to implement and fund. New models and having researchers aware of what costs to include in grants is an area that will be a challenge.

We interpret "keeping up with technology changes" as awareness of technology changes, not their actual implementation. If this question is about upgrading and maintaining systems to keep them current we would select 4.

We need additional resources and support to keep up with myriad needs in this space. In particular, we need a dedicated team, including people whose roles are specifically to curate datasets.

We would need to reassign staff and/or hire new positions to support full-scale data curation.

IMPORTANCE OF DATA CURATION SERVICES

While your library may not currently provide data curation services and treatments, the project team is interested in understanding which curation treatments you and your institution find important. The following sections will provide a list of treatments and definitions for five categories of data curation services. Please indicate the importance of these treatments along the specified spectrum.

INGEST ACTIVITIES

Here are descriptions of six data curation ingest activities.

Authentication: The process of confirming the identity of a person, generally the depositor, who is contributing data to the data repository. (e.g., password authentication or authorization via digital signature). Used for tracking provenance of the data files.

Chain of Custody: Intentional recording of provenance metadata of the files (e.g., metadata about who created the file, when it was last edited, etc.) in order to preserve file authenticity when data are transferred to third parties.

Deposit Agreement: The certification by the data author (or depositor) that the data conform to all policies and conditions (e.g., do not violate any legal restrictions placed on the data) and are fit for deposit into the repository. A deposit agreement may also include rights transfer to the repository for ongoing stewardship.

Documentation: Information describing any necessary information to use and understand the data. Documentation may be structured (e.g., a code book) or unstructured (e.g., a plain text "Readme" file).

File Validation: A computational process to ensure that the intended data transfer to a repository was perfect and complete using means such as generating and validating file checksums (e.g., test if a digital file has changed at the bit level) and format validation to ensure that file types match their extensions.

Metadata: Information about a data set that is structured (often in machine-readable format) for purposes of search and retrieval. Metadata elements may include basic information (e.g. title, author, date created, etc.) and/or specific elements inherent to datasets (e.g., spatial coverage, time periods).

36. **Please indicate the importance of these data curation ingest activities on a scale of 1 to 5 where 1=essential; 2=very important; 3=moderately important; 4=less important; 5=not important.** N=24

Activity	1	2	3	4	5	Rating Average
Metadata	18	6	0	0	0	1.25
Deposit agreement	14	8	2	0	0	1.50
Documentation	17	3	3	1	0	1.50
File validation	8	9	5	1	1	2.08
Authentication	10	5	5	3	1	2.17
Chain of custody	6	9	4	3	2	2.42
# of respondents	22	20	11	6	2	

Note: A lower average rating indicates a more important activity.

Comments N=5

All of these responses reflect importance in an ideal world (in which we had unlimited funds, personnel, time, etc.) In no way could our institution actually do this at scale.

All six of these items are important, but from an institutional priorities point of view (and of course limited time and resources), we have ranked these with current practice.

For a robust system with preservation as a mandate then these are all essential.

It isn't possible for us to comment on the importance of these activities. We have not had in-depth conversations about data curation at the library.

We tend to assume that the researcher/group will provide the best documentation and that our forte is metadata for discoverability. Deposit agreements are already part of the ingest workflow for articles, so would probably remain for data sets.

IMPORTANCE OF APPRAISAL ACTIVITIES

Here are descriptions of three data curation appraisal activities.

Rights Management: The process of tracking and managing ownership and copyright inherent to a data set as well as monitoring conditions and policies for access and reuse (e.g., licenses and data use agreements).

Risk Management: The process of reviewing data for known risks such as confidentiality issues inherent to human subjects data, sensitive information (e.g., sexual histories, credit card information) or data regulated by law (e.g., HIPAA, FERPA) and taking actions to reject or facilitate remediation (e.g., de-identification services) when necessary.

Selection: The result of a successful appraisal. The data are determined appropriate for acceptance and ingest into the repository according to local collection policy and practice.

37. **Please indicate the importance of these data curation appraisal activities on a scale of 1 to 5 where 1=essential; 2=very important; 3=moderately important; 4=less important; 5=not important.** N=24

Activity	1	2	3	4	5	Rating Average
Rights Management	14	8	1	1	0	1.54
Risk Management	10	7	3	2	1	2.00
Selection	4	10	5	4	1	2.50
# of respondents	18	20	8	6	1	

Note: A lower average rating indicates a more important activity.

Comments N=6

Although risk management and selection are important, this is currently not within our scope for thinking about data curation services. We recommend faculty go with more secure, discipline-specific repositories for sharing data with confidentiality issues. It is likely we would need substantial infrastructure (human and technology) to support more advanced activities. For selection, it would be wonderful to have both the staff and the infrastructure to appraise datasets, but it would also be beneficial to be able to have a back-and-forth with faculty to get faculty to an appropriate level. Our relationships with faculty are key!

Due to constrained resources, we are considering non-mediated deposit.

Risk management and selection are critical, but not for libraries to do.

There are some risks to the selection process but didn't seem as essential as the first two activities. Doing the first two activities reduces some of the risk for selection.

We feel like risk management and selection are essential, but we do not think that they are necessarily the responsibility of the data curation service.

We struggle with selection as a criteria. If we have the capacity to take data from one of our researchers, we will take it, unless there is another more appropriate repository for those data.

IMPORTANCE OF PROCESSING AND REVIEW ACTIVITIES PART 1

Here are descriptions of eight data curation processing and review activities.

Arrangement and Description: The re-organization of files (e.g., new folder directory structure) in a dataset that may also involve the creation of new file names, file descriptions, and the recording of technical metadata inherent to the files (e.g., date last modified).

Code Review: Run and validate computer code (e.g., look for missing files and/or errors) in order to find mistakes overlooked in the initial development phase, improving the overall quality of software.

Contextualize: Use metadata to link the data set to related publications, dissertations, and/or projects that provide added context to how the data were generated and why.

Conversion (Analog): In effort to increase the usability of a data set, the information is transferred into digital file formats (e.g., analog data keyed into a database). Note: digital conversion is also used to convert "fixed" data (e.g., PDF formats) into machine-readable formats.

Curation Log: A written record of any changes made to the data during the curation process and by whom. File is often preserved as part of the overall record.

Data Cleaning: A process used to improve data quality by detecting and correcting (or removing) defects & errors in data.

Deidentification: Redacting or removing personally identifiable or protected information (e.g., sensitive geographic locations) from a dataset prior to sharing with third parties.

File Format Transformations: Transform files into open, non-proprietary file formats that broaden the potential for long-term reuse and ensure that additional preservation actions might be taken in the future. Note: Retention of the original file formats may be necessary if data transfer is not perfect.

38. **Please indicate the importance of these data curation processing and reveiw activities on a scale of 1 to 5 where 1=essential; 2=very important; 3=moderately important; 4=less important; 5=not important.** N=23

Activity	1	2	3	4	5	Rating Average
File Format Transformations	10	5	5	3	0	2.04
Contextualize	8	8	5	1	1	2.09
Curation Log	9	5	4	1	3	2.27
Deidentification	10	3	6	1	3	2.30
Arrangement and Description	4	8	8	3	0	2.43
Code review	3	6	6	3	5	3.04
Conversion (Analog)	4	4	6	5	4	3.04
Data Cleaning	2	6	6	4	5	3.17
# of respondents	16	18	15	10	8	

Note: A lower average rating indicates a more important activity.

Comments N=9

At this time, we expect most of the data processing, cleaning, and formatting to be done prior to deposit.

Data cleaning and deidentification are critical, but not for libraries to do.

Education related to these activities should happen well before submission as part of the data management plan (DMP).

Items marked as not important in planning for our service are because we expect the depositor/PI to be performing these.

Some hesitation to modify data submitted by the researcher—although it may be value-added to clean the data, there is the worry that it would fundamentally alter the data, despite best intentions. We continue to advise and educate faculty on best practices.

Some of these actions warrant consultation or advice, but we do not think that they are responsibilities that the curation center should take upon itself.

The 5s listed here are more an indication of where we stand on staffing and technological capability, while knowing we intend to provide guidance on all these topics during the ingest process.

The need to convert data from analog to digital formats will depend on the assessed value of the particular data set in question. Data cleaning and deidentification are very important curation activities but should be performed by the data owners rather than the library curation staff.

We believe all this is important, just not things the LIBRARY needs to do or should do.

IMPORTANCE OF PROCESSING AND REVIEW ACTIVITIES PART 2

Here are descriptions of ten more data curation processing and review activities.

File Inventory or Manifest: The data files are inspected periodically and the number, file types (extensions), and file sizes of the data are understood and documented. Any missing, duplicate, or corrupt (e.g., unable to open) files are discovered.

File Renaming: To rename files in a dataset, often to standardize and/or reflect important metadata.

Indexing: Verify all metadata provided by the author and crosswalk to descriptive and administrative metadata compliant with a standard format for repository interoperability.

Interoperability: Formatting the data using a disciplinary standard for better integration with other datasets and/or systems.

Peer-review: The review of a data set by an expert with similar credentials and subject knowledge as the data creator for the purposes of validating the soundness and trustworthiness of the file contents.

Persistent Identifier: A URL (or Uniform Resource Locator) that is monitored by an authority to ensure a stable web location for consistent citation and long-term discoverability. Provides redirection when necessary (e.g., a Digital Object Identifier or DOI).

Quality Assurance: Ensure that all documentation and metadata are comprehensive and complete. Example actions might include: open and run the data files; inspect the contents in order to validate, clean, and/or enhance data for future use; look for missing documentation about codes used, the significance of "null" and "blank" values, or unclear acronyms.

Restructure: Organize and/or reformat poorly structured data files to clarify their meaning and importance.

Software Registry: Maintain copies of modern and obsolete versions of software (and any relevant code libraries) so that data may be opened/used overtime.

Transcoding: With audio and video files, detect technical metadata (min resolution, audio/video codec) and encode files in ways that optimize reuse and long-term preservation actions (e.g., Convert QuickTime files to MPEG4).

39. **Please indicate the importance of these data curation processing and reveiw activities on a scale of 1 to 5 where 1=essential; 2=very important; 3=moderately important; 4=less important; 5=not important.** N=22

Activity	1	2	3	4	5	Rating Average
Persistent Identifier	18	3	1	0	0	1.23
File Inventory or Manifest	10	5	3	2	2	2.14
Indexing	6	8	5	2	1	2.27
Quality Assurance	3	9	6	2	2	2.59
Transcoding	4	9	3	4	2	2.59
Software Registry	2	8	5	5	2	2.86

Activity	1	2	3	4	5	Rating Average
File renaming	2	6	8	4	2	2.91
Interoperability	4	3	8	4	3	2.95
Restructure	1	5	8	5	3	3.18
Peer-review	0	2	6	6	8	3.91
# of respondents	18	20	19	14	9	

Note: A lower average rating indicates a more important activity.

Comments N=6

A software registry may be better at a consortial level rather than an individual institution.

Again, many of these are the responsibility of the researcher, not the librarian.

Again, these are all important activities, but would require significant investment in infrastructure from the campus. Here, we are weighting what is important to our campus in terms of what can theoretically be achieved in the coming years.

Software registry and transcoding, while important, are not often feasible. There is not a lot of available expertise.

The need for a software registry decreases if open/non-proprietary formats are used.

We see many of these as requirements for the system or for the depositor.

IMPORTANCE OF ACCESS ACTIVITIES

Here are descriptions of eleven data curation access activities.

Contact Information: Keep up-to-date contact information for the data authors and/or the contact persons in order to facilitate connection with third-party users. Often involves managing ephemeral information that will change over time.

Data Citation: Display of a recommended bibliographic citation for a dataset to enable appropriate attribution by third-party users in order to formally incorporate data reuse as part of the scholarly ecosystem.

Data Visualization: The presentation of pictorial and/or graphical representations of a data set used to identify patterns, detect errors, and/or demonstrate the extent of a data set to third party users.

Discovery Services: Services that incorporate machine-based search and retrieval functionality that help users identify what data exist, where the data are located, and how can they be accessed (e.g., full-text indexing or web optimization).

Embargo: To restrict or mediate access to a data set, usually for a set period of time. In some cases an embargo may be used to protect not only access, but any knowledge that the data exist.

File Download: Allow access to the data materials by authorized third parties.

Full-Text Indexing: Enhance the data for discovery purposes by generating search-engine-optimized formats of the text inherent to the data.

Metadata Brokerage: Active dissemination of a data set's metadata to search and discovery services (e.g., article databases, catalogs, web-based indexes) for federated search and discovery.

Restricted Access: In order to maintain the privacy of research subjects without losing integral components of the data, some data access will be protected and/or mediated to individuals that meet predefined criteria.

Terms of Use: Information provided to end users of a data set that outline the requirements or conditions for use (e.g., a Creative Commons License).

Use Analytics: Monitor and record how often data are viewed, requested, and/or downloaded. Track and report reuse metrics, such as data citations and impact measures for the data over time.

40. **Please indicate the importance of these data curation access activities on a scale of 1 to 5 where 1=essential; 2=very important; 3=moderately important; 4=less important; 5=not important.** N=23

Activity	1	2	3	4	5	Rating Average
Terms of Use	16	6	1	0	0	1.35
File download	16	5	2	0	0	1.39
Discovery Services	11	10	2	0	0	1.61
Data Citation	10	11	2	0	0	1.65
Embargo	7	10	5	1	0	2.00
Use Analytics	6	12	3	2	0	2.04
Metadata Brokerage	5	12	5	0	1	2.13
Restricted Access	8	6	4	3	1	2.23
Full-Text Indexing	5	9	5	1	3	2.48
Contact Information	4	7	4	5	3	2.83
Data Visualization	0	3	8	8	4	3.57
# of respondents	18	22	20	13	6	

Note: A lower average rating indicates a more important activity.

Comments N=5

Contact information is not important as long as good metadata is created that identifies the data creators.

Contact Information, while important, is essentially infeasible over the life of a data set. People move, retire, die, etc.

Most of these functions are already provided for articles in our IR, so extending them as features for a data repository are part of the plan.

These could have all been listed as essential.

Use analytics are possibly not absolutely essential, but they do show value and help make the case for deposit.

IMPORTANCE OF PRESERVATION ACTIVITIES

Here are descriptions of nine data curation preservation activities.

Cease Data Curation: Plan for any contingencies that will ultimately terminate access to the data. For example, providing tombstones or metadata records for data that have been deselected and removed from stewardship.

Emulation: Provide legacy system configurations in modern equipment in order to ensure long-term usability of data (e.g., arcade games emulated on modern web-browsers)

File Audit: Periodic review of the digital integrity of the data files and taking action when needed to protect data from digital erosion (e.g., bitrot) and/or hardware failure.

Migration: Monitor and anticipate file format obsolescence and, as needed, transform obsolete file formats to new formats as standards and use dictate.

Repository Certification: The technical and administrative capacities of the repository undergo review through a transparent and well-documented process by a trusted third-party accreditation body (e.g., TRAC, or Data Seal of Approval).

Secure Storage: Data files are properly stored in a well-configured (in terms of hardware and software) storage environment that is routinely backed-up and physically protected. Perform routine fixity checks (to detect degradation or loss) and provide recovery services as needed.

Succession Planning: Planning for contingency, and/or escrow arrangements, in the case that the repository (or other entity responsible) ceases to operate or the institution substantially changes its scope.

Technology Monitoring and Refresh: Formal, periodic review and assessment to ensure responsiveness to technological developments and evolving requirements of the digital infrastructure and hardware storing the data.

Versioning: Provide mechanisms to ingest new versions of the data overtime that includes metadata describing the version history and any changes made for each version.

41. **Please indicate the importance of these data curation preservation activities on a scale of 1 to 5 where 1=essential; 2=very important; 3=moderately important; 4=less important; 5=not important.** N=23

Activity	1	2	3	4	5	Rating Average
Secure Storage	16	4	2	0	1	1.52
File Audit	12	4	4	2	1	1.96
Versioning	10	7	4	0	2	2.00
Succession Planning	9	7	4	1	2	2.13
Technology Monitoring and Refresh	7	7	6	0	3	2.35
Migration	7	5	7	1	3	2.48
Cease Data Curation	5	7	6	3	2	2.57
Repository Certification	3	5	9	2	4	2.96
Emulation	1	6	3	7	6	3.48
# of respondents	18	18	15	9	7	

Note: A lower average rating indicates a more important activity.

Comments N=4

Emulation and repository certification are important, but not everyone needs to achieve this level.

Some of these will probably be the responsibility of central IT.

Succession planning is absolutely essential.

TRAC certification is important, but having the certification is not essential.

ADDITIONAL COMMENTS

42. **Please enter any additional information regarding data curation practices at your institution that may assist the authors in accurately analyzing the results of this survey.** N=34

Currently provide data curation services N=20

2012–2016 we were using Hydra/Fedora as a data repository. Starting in March 2016, we moved to local installation of Dataverse.

Data curation is not centralized, and the institution is currently reviewing policy with respect to research datasets. There are multiple sites of data curation within the university, this survey response has attempted to capture those from the University Library System and the Health Sciences Library System, but does include other centers and units.

Due to our small staff size we focus on automated data curation workflow development to achieve efficiencies for ingesting large collections of data. We are currently in the process of establishing the necessary relationships with campus IT and the Office of the Vice President for Research to address scalability and outreach needs. Significant organizational turnover in IT, OVPR, and library IT have also posed challenges to establishing scalable systems in support of data curation.

I have a growing sense that our community's data curation programs are neither here nor there. That is, attempts to curate data with a high degree of interaction with researchers (e.g., for preservation purposes) have resulted in low amounts of data deposit. Most researchers do not understand the need for such effort. Alternately, strategies that result in greater data deposit may be compromising the ability to preserve data in the future (with "future" being defined as little as five years). Much of our data curation activity relates to compliance with funding agency guidelines or requirements. Is this resulting in a coordinated, intentional collection effort? Is it resulting in better research? Reproducibility of research? Are libraries providing data curation for the large reference collections of data? Regardless of your political view, the reality is that many researchers are currently exerting effort to safeguard, transfer, migrate, etc. their data given the current political climate. How many of them are reaching out to ARL libraries for help? If the answer is not many—or even none—shouldn't we ask ourselves why?

More on the "above campus" activity: consortial and commercial arrangements that impact policy and procedural developments.

Most of our current/to date support for data curation comes in the form of consultations for DMPs. We do have more robust data curation for our special collections. We do not have a data repository at this time. Should this situation change, we would embark on more data curation activities.

NARA is a federal agency responsible for preserving and providing access to electronic records scheduled for permanent retention in the National Archives. Our legislative mandate and supporting regulations and guidance require federal agencies to transfer records in regular intervals, in acceptable formats, and with adequate documentation and metadata.

One of the challenges is being able to re-allocate resources to data curation when new funding is not available. Mandates for depositing research data are not very strong yet in Canada, and demand for data curation services is not always high enough to drive funding. UBC is one of the leaders of Portage, a Canadian, library-based research data management network that coalesces initiatives in research data management to build capacity and to coordinate activities (https://portagenetwork.ca/about/).

Our Data Coordinating Center provides many of these services, however, they are part of our CTSI and the library is currently developing a relationship with them (thus it is hard to provide exact information). Also, some questions feel library-centric and while some of these services are being provided, I'm not sure if the providers would use the same language to describe their work.

Our practices and support/resources are evolving rapidly. None of this might represent our services two years from now. The repository will still be here, but might look very different.

Our responses represent our efforts to launch a new and greatly enhanced set of services in this area. We recently brought on four new staff members to support data curation, so our numbers for staff may seem distorted with respect to the amount of data we currently have in our IR. Many of our responses reflect our plans to begin rolling out and advertising new services in the current calendar year.

Our situation is affected by the recent addition of a self-deposit institutional repository into the mix. Currently, we have two workflows for curating research data, 1) completely mediated by staff in Repository & Data Curation for large sets of audio or visual data and 2) the self-deposit institutional repository for research data supporting publication.

See websites for the Research Data unit of our Libraries, http://www.lib.purdue.edu/researchdata, as well as PURR, http://purr.purdue.edu (in particular, its policies and knowledge base). Also, we have tried to publish and present our experience in designing and implementing data services at Purdue in the literature and conferences.

The University Library formally rolled out Research Data Services in 2016 to the campus and have had a data curation librarian for a little over a year. There are not many positions out there that explicitly address data curation (in libraries). We anticipate growth in the role and instantiation of other services in the library that will compliment it and integrate it into our other systems. So, we anticipate the need to grow expertise in digital preservation and curation generally as a critical need.

There are a few complicating factors to our responses to this survey: 1) Our services for end-users in this area are just emerging and quite minimal in many ways. Changes to our technical infrastructure will impact the shape and extent of our services going forward. 2) Curation services are dispersed among several different units within the libraries and alongside affiliated services in other units (for example, university IT, the Center for Urban Science and Progress, etc.), so getting a complete picture is challenging (maybe that in itself is data!) 3) We are developing similar processes for end-user created and division of libraries curated data, and in some cases, resources may start in the former category but move to the latter category over time, and in that process receive enhanced curation attention. Answering this survey becomes quite difficult in these cases. 4) Getting firm numbers of submissions into our various repositories, and deciding which meet the definition of being "data sets" (numeric? geospatial? curated moving image files? born-digital special collections?) was very difficult.

We are in the early stages of developing data curation services.

We are in the process of moving our datasets from Islandora (e-Scholarship repository) to the campus instance of Dataverse. From 2016, datasets appear in both; in future, datasets will be held in Dataverse alone, but with a record (linking out to the content in Dataverse) in Islandora.

We are just starting to look at data curation and have just opened up our institutional repository. We are in the beginning phases of exploring what is needed by the faculty and the role the library should play in that process beyond simply providing a data store that faculty can use.

We are selective about the data projects we accept for deposit. Some data curation activities might not result in data deposit.

While we may not have all the cyberinfrastructure in place to fully offer an institutional repository with all the features, the library staff is still working with researchers to help instill the idea of best practices, documentation, preservation (at a lab group or center) to help insure their data will be ready. Outside providers through granting agencies, domain centers, and such are still where we are actively supporting the research mission of the researchers here on campus. The issue is determining what level of archiving and curation digital assets (data sets) we will need. Not all can be given the additional support, but still need to be made available and have a minimum level of documentation, metadata, and care. As the amount of data grows, this becomes less of an individual problem and more of a national one. Not all libraries are equipped with expertise and infrastructures to support at this time a robust repository. Instead of all of the institutions striking out on their own, maybe it is time for a more federated approach, building locally what will help scale regionally and nationally.

Do not provide data curation services N=5

Currently, our liaison libraries aid faculty members through education of repositories available, including OCUL Scholars Portal Dataverse, and giving advice on metadata. The DMP should guide the researcher through the process and we are available for assistance. Our answers to the "importance of" questions are based on an assumption of long-term preservation. Collection policies and retention guidelines are key to a local service.

Data curation is still very much in the beginning stages at our organization. While we have an agreement with bePress, we have a long way to go towards deeper curation of researcher data!

We do not currently have a data curation program. We will be developing a program in the near future.

While we currently have some supplementary datasets in our institutional repository (i.e., data that is associated with an article and submitted as a supplementary file), we do not have an active data curation program. We are currently considering the libraries' position and this may change in the future.

While we have not had in-depth discussions about data curation at the library, we do value many of the above concepts (persistent identifiers, analytics, embargoes, discovery services) as they apply to our institutional repository. But data curation is not within the library's purview. There is, however, a group on campus called Academic Resource Computing, a division of University Information Services. They provide some custodial and data storage services for faculty, mostly for the medical school.

Data curation services are in process N=9

I have said we are in process although we are beginning to ingest data into our IR and offer very preliminary services. I'm not ready to call that active yet, however!

Importance of data curation activities are rated with respect to our current "in process" state. Research data curation services are rated as "in process"; no documents or web pages are currently available.

Most of our activities in this area are in development, and most likely will be significantly more clear in the next 6–12 months.

Our responses reflect our most recent initiative and activity. We began offering data curation services in 2016; thus far, we have not received any requests. That said, our archival branches of the library have slightly different approaches to data curation that are not reflected in our responses to this survey.

Our updated repository in in the process of being constructed.

Please note that we are in planning stages of this practice, and many of these aspects have not yet been considered.

We have completed workshops for graduate students that focused on general data management and curation information. We offer a repository for research data through the Texas Digital Library's Texas Data Repository (http://data.tdl.org).

We are in the initial stages of developing and deploying a RDM and RDC program in the libraries. It is expected to be an area of significant attention and investment in the next few years.

While we think all these activities are ultimately very important, we think these activities should be handled in collaboration with other campus offices and the researcher themselves.

Responding Institutions

University of Alabama

University of Alberta

Arizona State University

Boston University

Boston College

Brigham Young University

University of British Columbia

University of Calgary

University of California, Irvine

University of California, Los Angeles

University of California, Santa Barbara

Case Western Reserve University

University of Colorado at Boulder

Colorado State University

University of Connecticut

Cornell University

University of Delaware

Duke University

Emory University

University of Florida

Florida State University

Georgetown University

Georgia Institute of Technology

University of Guelph

University of Houston

University of Illinois at Chicago

University of Illinois at Urbana-Champaign

University of Iowa

Iowa State University

Johns Hopkins University

University of Kansas

University of Kentucky

Université Laval

University of Louisville

McGill University

University of Maryland

University of Massachusetts, Amherst

University of Miami

University of Michigan

Michigan State University

University of Minnesota

National Archives and Records Administration

University of Nebraska—Lincoln

University of New Mexico

New York University

University of North Carolina at Chapel Hill

North Carolina State University

Northwestern University

University of Notre Dame

Ohio State University

University of Oklahoma

Oklahoma State University

University of Oregon

University of Pennsylvania

Pennsylvania State University

University of Pittsburgh

Purdue University

Rice University

Rutgers University

University of South Carolina

University at Albany, SUNY

University at Buffalo, SUNY

Syracuse University

Temple University

University of Tennessee

University of Texas at Austin

University of Toronto

Tulane University

Vanderbilt University

University of Virginia

Virginia Tech

University of Washington

Washington State University

Washington University in St. Louis

University of Waterloo

Wayne State University

Western University

University of Wisconsin—Madison

Yale University

York University

Representative Documents

Data Repositories

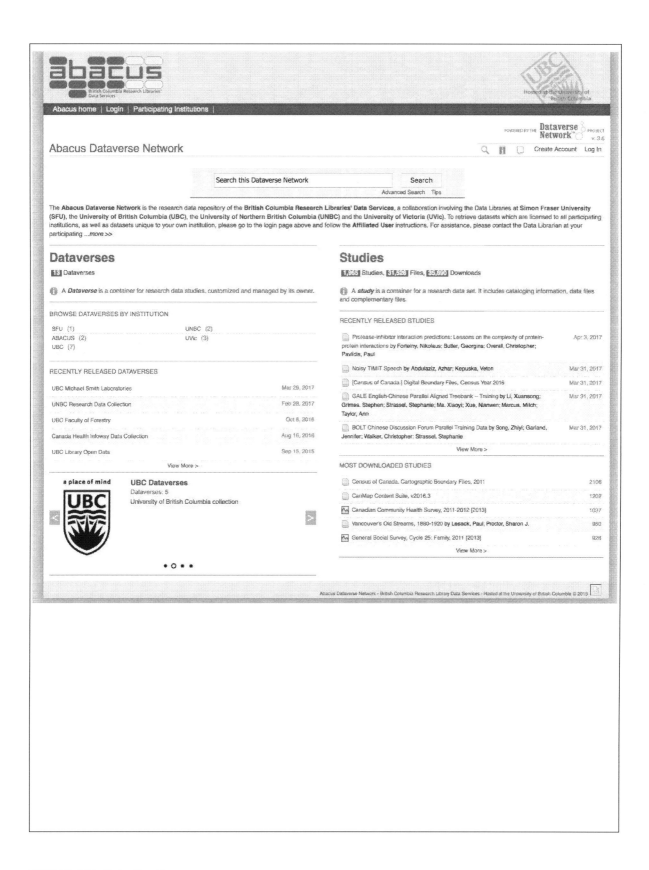

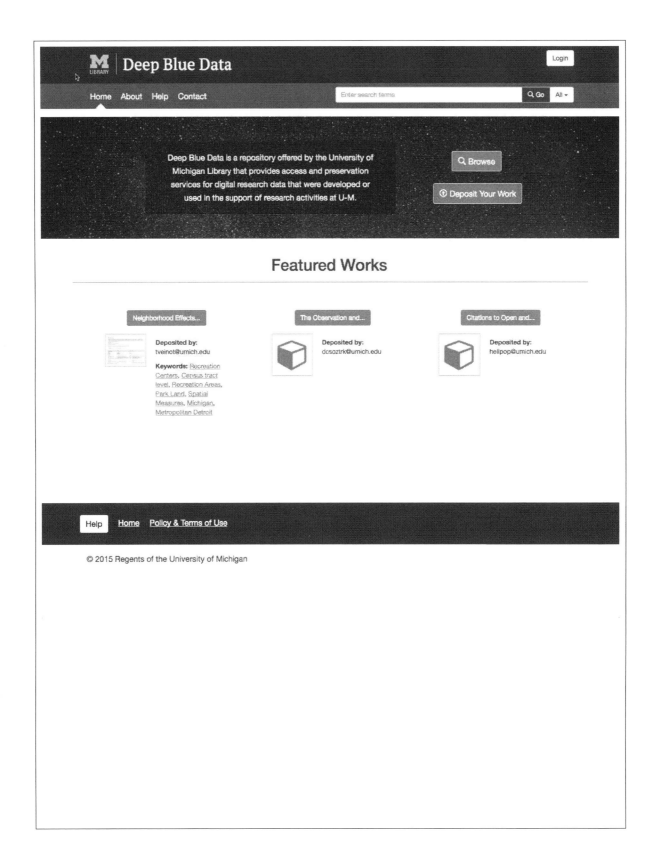

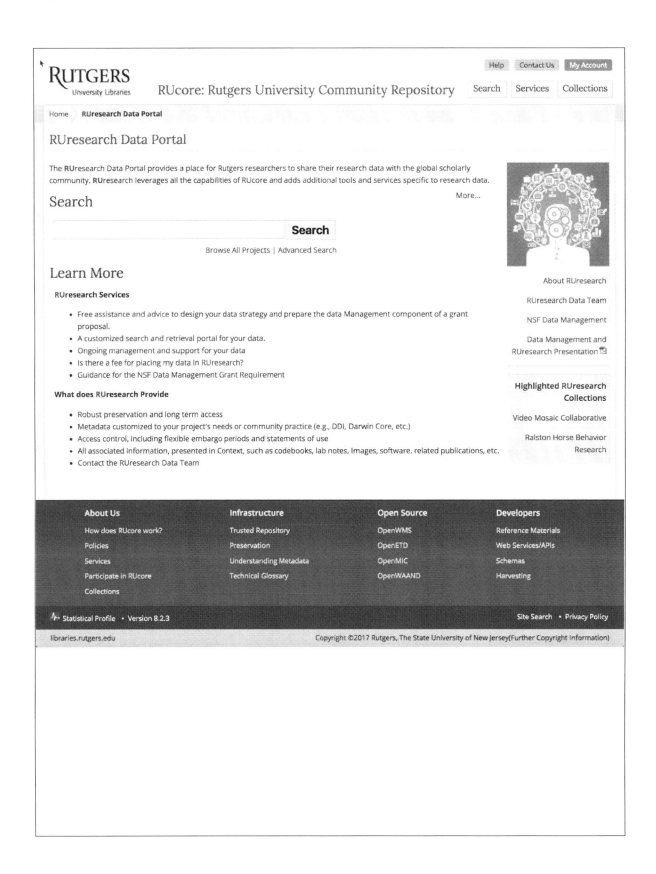

SCHOLARS PORTAL
Dataverse
https://dataverse.scholarsportal.info/

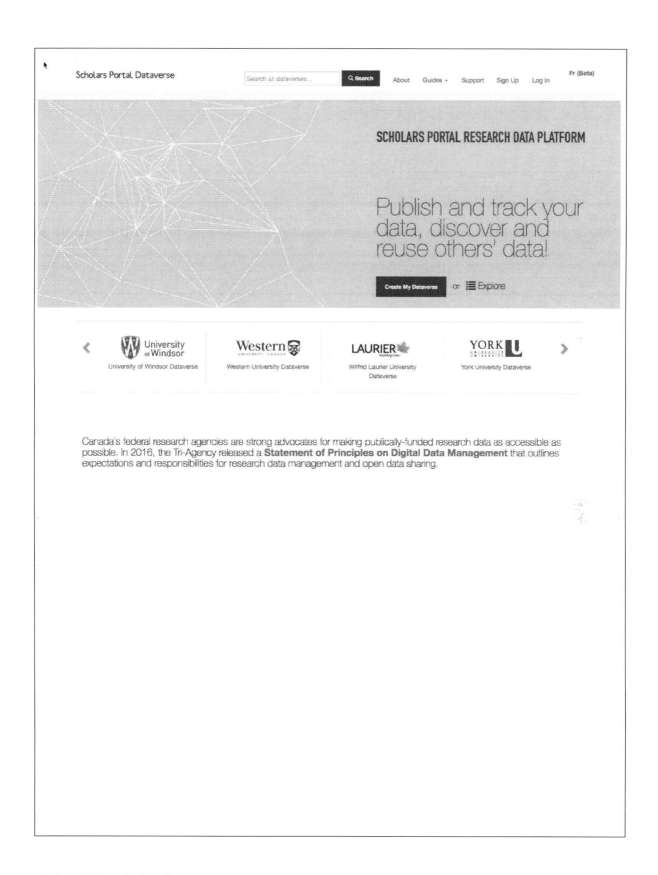

 Texas Digital Library

search here ...   Go

HOME   ABOUT   NEWS   MEMBERS   SERVICES   TRAINING   SUPPORT

Home › Texas Data Repository

Texas Data Repository

The Texas Data Repository is a platform for publishing and archiving datasets (and other data products) created by faculty, staff, and students at Texas higher education institutions. The repository (https://dataverse.tdl.org/) is built in an open-source application called Dataverse, developed and used by Harvard University.

The repository is hosted by the Texas Digital Library, a consortium of academic libraries in Texas with a proven history of providing shared technology services that support secure, reliable access to digital collections of research and scholarship.

Benefits of a Texas Data Repository

- **Compliance with funding requirements.** The Texas Data Repository helps researchers comply with funder mandates for data archiving and sharing, and supports research grant-seekers by having infrastructure available at the time of proposal.
- **Reliable, managed access for data.** The Texas Data Repository provides a convenient and reliable place to collect and share data. And by depositing data there, researchers benefit from the Texas Digital Library's focus on long-term access and preservation of scholarly content.
- **Increase scholarly impact.** By publishing their data in the Texas Data Repository, researchers give their data credibility through a unique, citable, and persistent online identifier (i.e., a Digital Object Identifier), which makes it easy for others to cite reliably.
- **Collaboration with research teams.** Some situations may necessitate restricting access to data, at least for a period of time. The Texas Data Repository allows researchers to share their data with a select group of colleagues, version the data, and publish it when they're ready.
- **Access to local support through their institution's library.** Along with robust technical support from the TDL, users of the Texas Data Repository can rely on trained librarians at their home institution to assist with multiple phases of the research cycle, including data management planning preparation for data publishing, and long-term curation.
- **Efficient use of resources.** By pooling resources across multiple institutions, the Texas Data Repository realizes cost savings through a shared infrastructure while showcasing local contributions through university-branded data collections and local library services. Each institution can focus its resources on unique services that meet local research community needs.

How the Texas Data Repository Works

The Texas Data Repository is designed for regular to mid-sized data sets (individual file sizes up to 2 GB), which comprises the majority of research data. These data can include:

- Data from any scholarly discipline and in any file type
- Materials such as codebooks and other supplementary documentation
- Data that does NOT contain confidential or sensitive information (like social security numbers or other identifiers)

Researchers affiliated with participating TDL member institutions will be able to:

- Store and organize data sets and upload files
- Maintain multiple versions data sets
- Share data sets online with trusted colleagues OR release data for public access online
- Get recognition and proper academic credit for scholarly work through a data citation with a persistent identifier (i.e., a DOI, or digital object identifier)

Library faculty or staff at each of TDL's participating member institutions will provide local assistance to researchers at their institution as they prepare and deposit their data.

- Each participating university will have its own branded "dataverse" within the overall repository, which it can use to showcase its researcher contributions.

Participate in the Texas Data Repository

Institutions interested in participating in the Texas Data Repository must be an institution of higher learning in Texas and a member of the Texas Digital Library. To find out more about membership opportunities, please see the Membership section of our website.

If your TDL member institution decides to participate, all faculty, staff, and students at your institution will be able to deposit their datasets. Anyone may view or download datasets in the Texas Data Repository, but only individuals from a participating TDL member institution may deposit datasets.

TDL members should contact the TDL (info@tdl.org) to begin utilizing this new service. The process includes:

- Sign a Memorandum of Understanding
- Establish authentication systems on your campus (e.g., Shibboleth or Two Factor)
- Identify a Texas Data Repository liaison on your campus

Contact   Policies   State of Texas   Web Accessibility Policy

© 2017 Default copyright text

VIRGINIA TECH UNIVERSITY LIBRARIES
VTechData
https://data.lib.vt.edu/

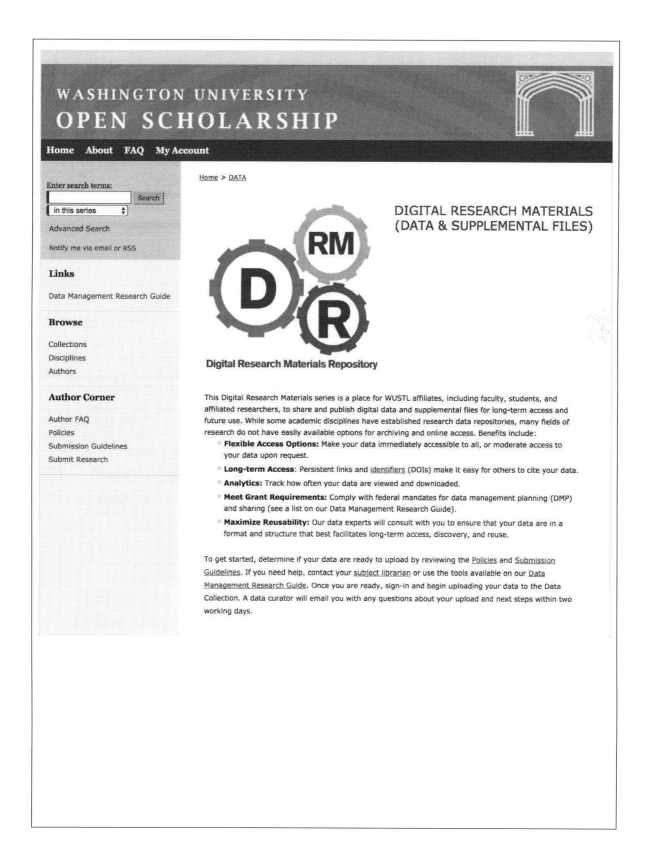

Data Curation Services

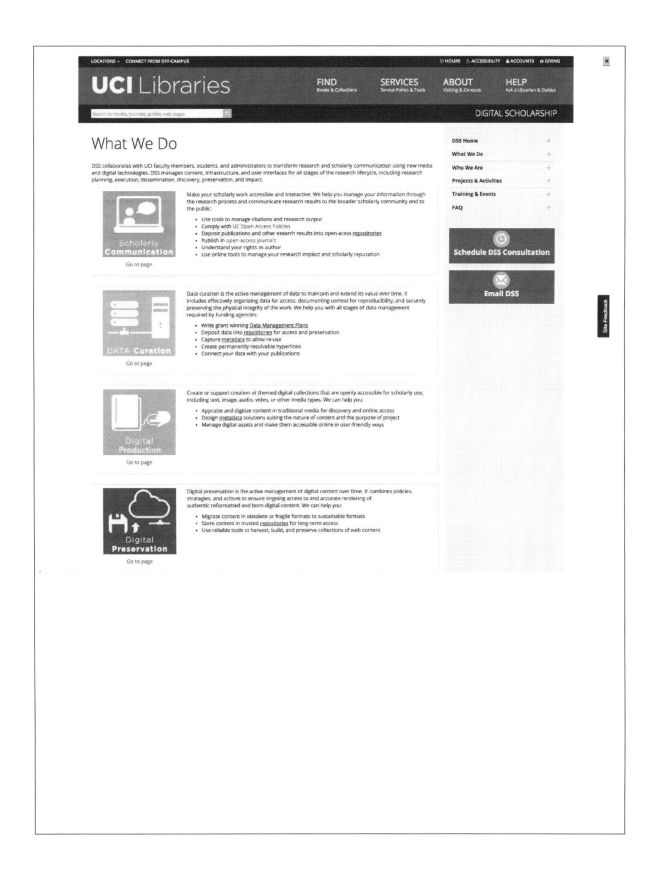

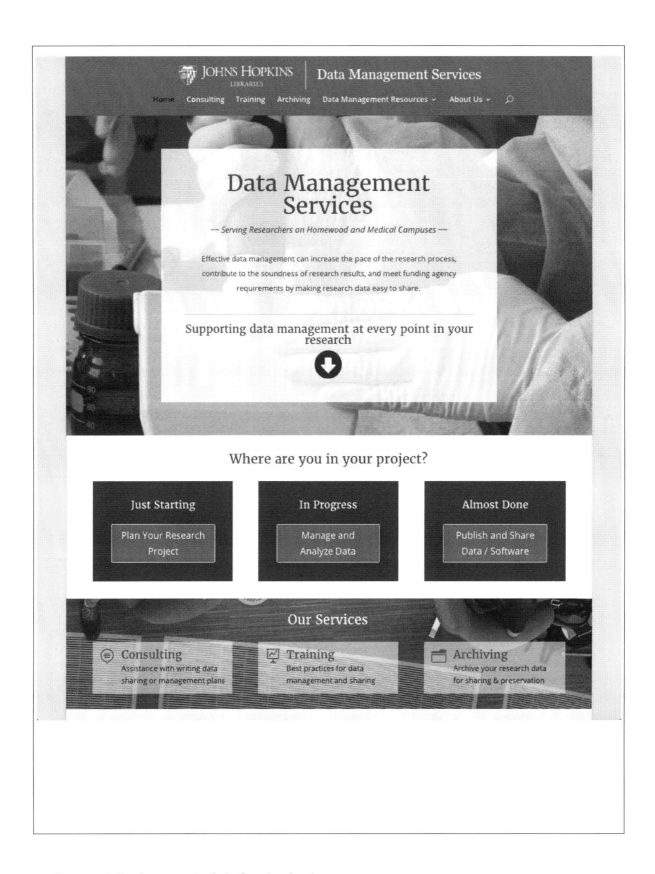

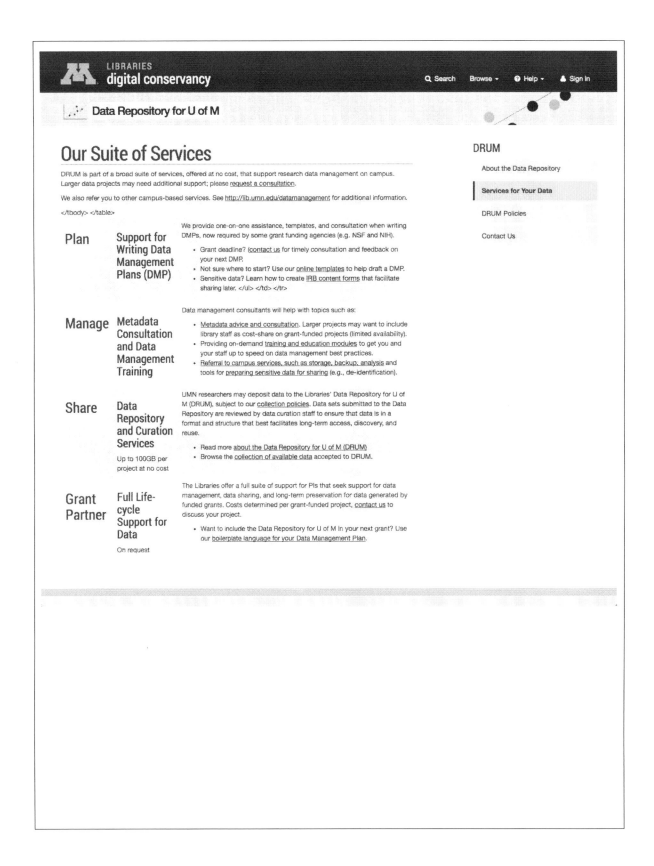

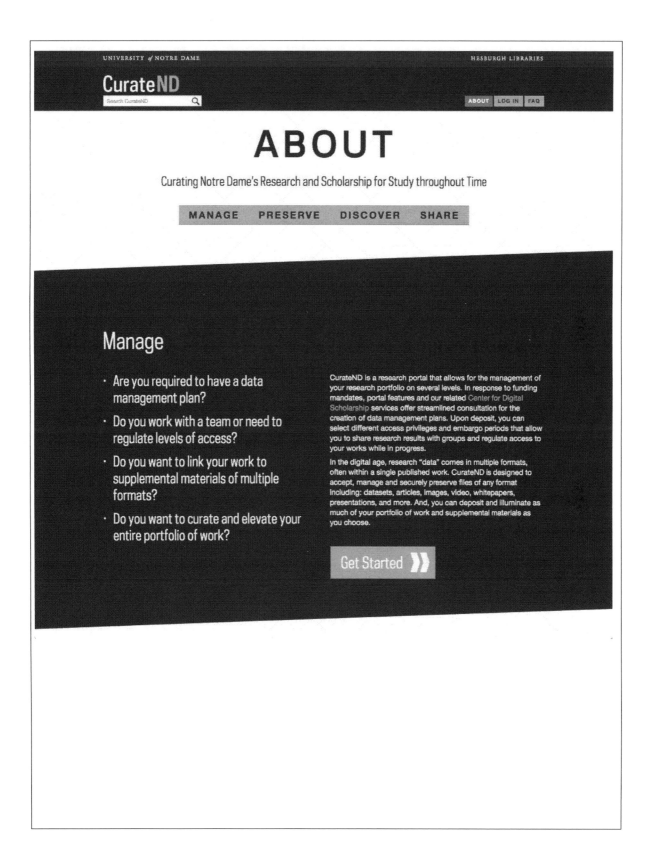

MANAGE   PRESERVE   DISCOVER   SHARE

Preserve

· Does your funding mandate a plan for long-term preservation?

· Do you want assurances that you can locate your research and related works in the future?

· Do you want to preserve conference proceedings?

· Is it important to steward your research for future scientists and scholars?

CurateND employs preservation standards that meet the requirements of funding agencies for long-term preservation and curation over the life-cycle of research. Whether or not a project is grant-funded, our preservation standards will give you security and peace of mind that you will find your work in the future and it will be guarded against corruption.

And, should the need arise, the platform will migrate files to new formats for continued access and usability. All this is to ensure that your work and the work of your students is preserved for future study throughout time.

Get Started ❯❯

MANAGE   PRESERVE   DISCOVER   SHARE

Share

· Are you required to share your research, data and related works?

· Do you need to create a DOI for citing and sharing your data?

· Do you have images, posters, presentations, collections, white papers or datasets that you want to share?

· Do you want to highlight the work of graduate and undergraduate research?

For those with grant-funded research and data sharing mandates, CurateND puts your front-end data management plan into action. You have the ability (rights not withstanding) to share content at any level—from restricted access, to lab or campus access, to open access for the world.

CurateND can create a DOI on demand, linking to works on your behalf. A DOI is a convenient (and often required) way to cite your data in publications and it makes it easy for others to cite your work. You can share all of the associated work and multiple data formats that are not supported by the publishing platform.

It is equally valuable for featuring the important contributions of undergraduate and graduate research across all disciplines. All members of the campus community can create an account and contribute to intellectual fabric that is Notre Dame.

Get Started »

UNIVERSITY OF
NOTRE DAME
Hesburgh Libraries

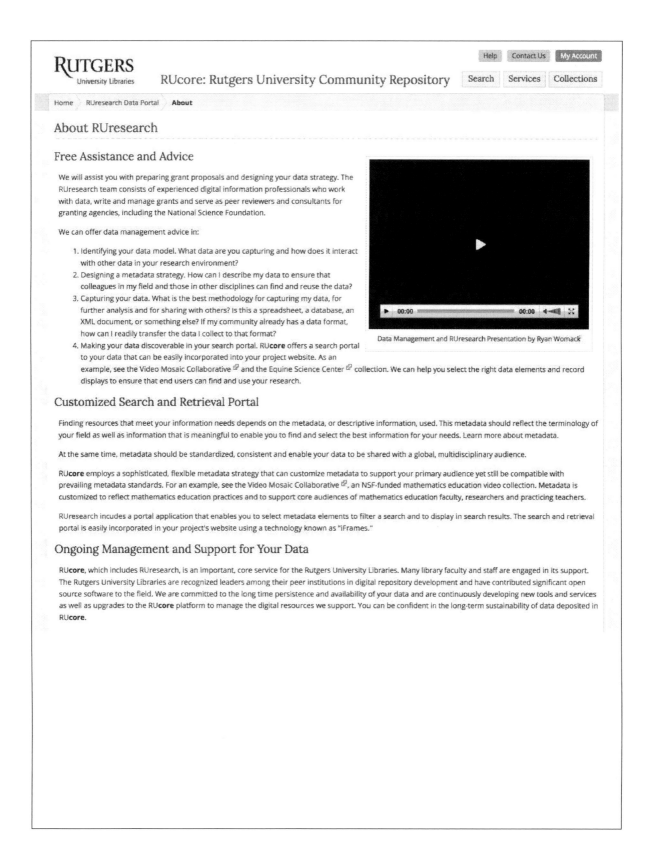

RUTGERS
University Libraries

RUcore: Rutgers University Community Repository

Help   Contact Us   My Account

Search   Services   Collections

Home › RUresearch Data Portal › **About**

Is there a fee for placing my data in RUresearch?

RU**core** accepts all types of resources that represent the significant intellectual output of the university. This includes faculty journal articles and other scholarly publications, theses and dissertations for degrees awarded by Rutgers University, and resources such as data sets that result from the research process. Individual resources, such as individual data sets that involve simple cataloging and storage, such as the example data sets currently available in the RUresearch portal, can be accepted at no cost. The same is true for electronic journal article preprints and post prints.

The Library will consult on your data management plan or grant at no cost, but managing data for a large research project , such as projects generally funded by grants, involves significant work and planning that will generally require a fee for service. The services we offer include customizing metadata and providing both ongoing cataloging and storage and management of data and associated documents and software. This fee can be accommodated through cost recovery charges in the grant budget, either as a data management fee or through the involvement of library faculty and staff as co-P.I.s or researchers on the grant, with associated line item cost recovery. This will be a one-time, cost recovery only fee that can be incorporated into the grant proposal budget. Data will be preserved and made accessible for the long term at no additional cost to the project beyond the one-time initial cost. However, that initial cost, although negotiable, will be based on the amount of work and effort anticipated for the life of the project.

Robust Preservation

The Rutgers University Libraries' RU**core** initiative includes a Data Curation Research Center and a Data Curator who participates actively in digital preservation research and development. The Rutgers University Libraries are internationally recognized as being on the forefront for digital preservation standards and practices, particularly for digital video. We currently employ "industry best practices" for digital file preservation, including:

Data Curation Research Center

- Multiple backups and restoration practices, including online, nearline, off line and offsite storage of files.
- Continuous file integrity checks, such as checksum assignment and checking
- Persistent identifiers that use metadata to continuously locate a file, even if it is moved during routine storage reallocation. When you reference a citation URL, you can be confident that the file will be retrieved.
- Storage of files in multiple formats. One or more canonical formats that are vendor independent and conform to non-proprietary standards are employed whenever feasible. The original file format is also always maintained. We are currently transcoding most numeric data sets to comma separated values (CSV) format. We are also currently investigating XML (eXtensible Markup Language) and RDF (Resource Description Framework) for web based canonical formats, as well as community specific data standards such as the DDI (Data Documentation Initiative) for social science and survey data, and SensorML for sensor data. If your community uses a specific data storage format, we will explore its use with you.

Learn more about preservation

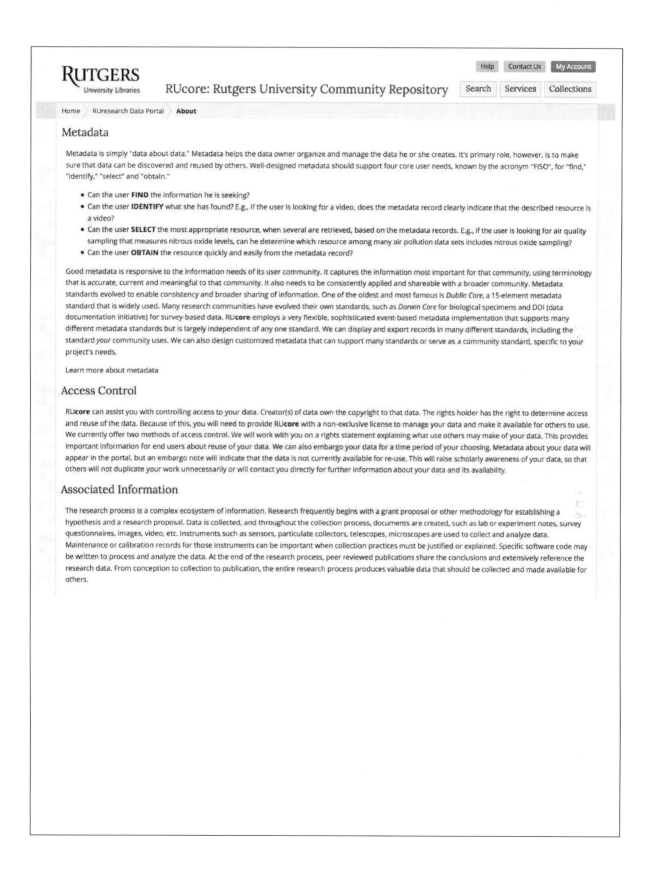

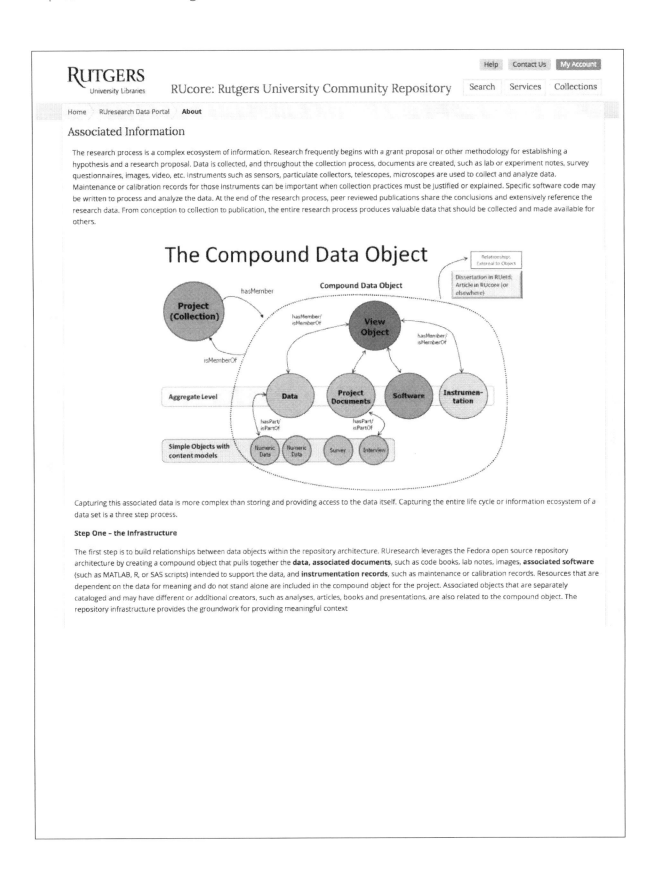

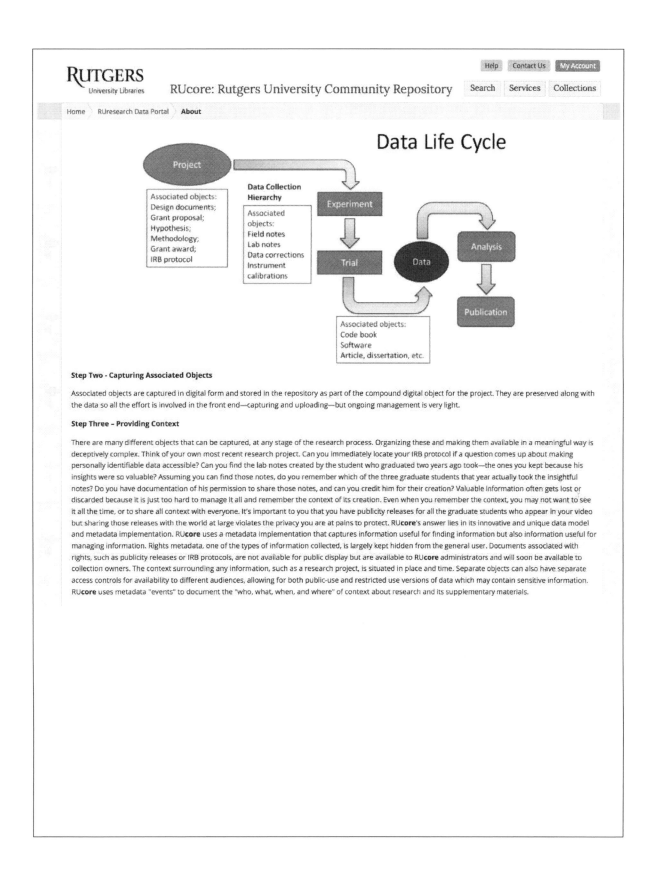

Step Two - Capturing Associated Objects

Associated objects are captured in digital form and stored in the repository as part of the compound digital object for the project. They are preserved along with the data so all the effort is involved in the front end—capturing and uploading—but ongoing management is very light.

Step Three – Providing Context

There are many different objects that can be captured, at any stage of the research process. Organizing these and making them available in a meaningful way is deceptively complex. Think of your own most recent research project. Can you immediately locate your IRB protocol if a question comes up about making personally identifiable data accessible? Can you find the lab notes created by the student who graduated two years ago took—the ones you kept because his insights were so valuable? Assuming you can find those notes, do you remember which of the three graduate students that year actually took the insightful notes? Do you have documentation of his permission to share those notes, and can you credit him for their creation? Valuable information often gets lost or discarded because it is just too hard to manage it all and remember the context of its creation. Even when you remember the context, you may not want to see it all the time, or to share all context with everyone. It's important to you that you have publicity releases for all the graduate students who appear in your video but sharing those releases with the world at large violates the privacy you are at pains to protect. RU**core**'s answer lies in its innovative and unique data model and metadata implementation. RU**core** uses a metadata implementation that captures information useful for finding information but also information useful for managing information. Rights metadata, one of the types of information collected, is largely kept hidden from the general user. Documents associated with rights, such as publicity releases or IRB protocols, are not available for public display but are available to RU**core** administrators and will soon be available to collection owners. The context surrounding any information, such as a research project, is situated in place and time. Separate objects can also have separate access controls for availability to different audiences, allowing for both public-use and restricted use versions of data which may contain sensitive information. RU**core** uses metadata "events" to document the "who, what, when, and where" of context about research and its supplementary materials.

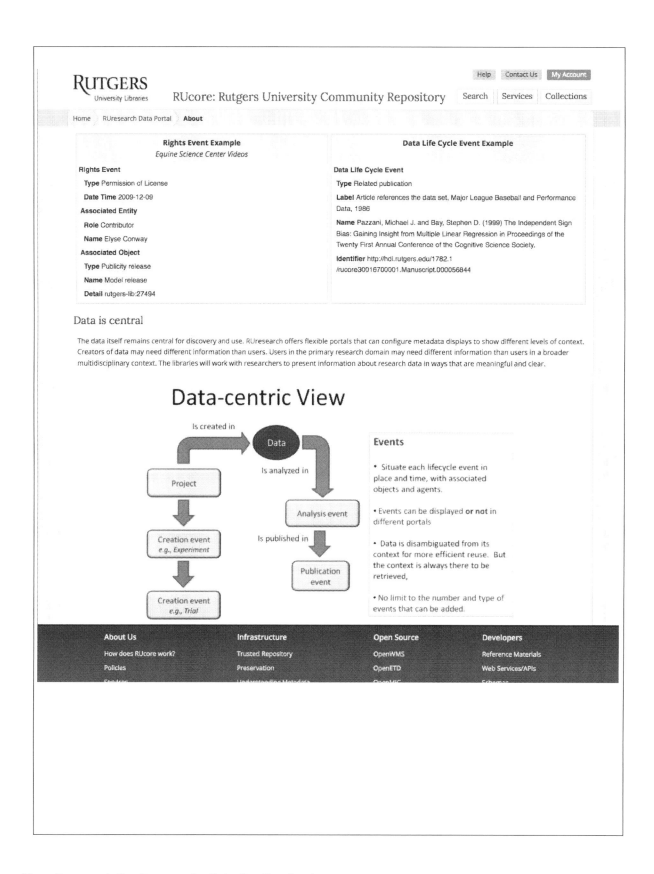

VirginiaTech *Invent the Future®* | *VTechData*

Search VTechData...   [🔍] [All ▾]   [→ Login]

HOME   ABOUT   **HELP**   **CONTACT**

Virginia Tech's Data Repository (VTechData) is a platform for openly publishing datasets or other research products created by Virginia Tech faculty, staff, and students.

Content Policy

The purpose of VTechData is to highlight, preserve, and provide access to work produced by the Virginia Tech community and the intellectual output of the university in its land-grant mission. VTechData and Virginia Tech serve the Commonwealth of Virginia, the nation, and the world's community through the discovery and dissemination of new knowledge.

Data and associated materials will be accepted in any language and in a variety of forms and formats. Through the deposit process, depositors are encouraged to provide adequate documentation to ensure usability and accessibility, and should include discipline-specific documentation in a separate file, where appropriate. VTechData staff may be able to provide some of these services.

VTechData Publication and Curation services include:
- minting DOIs for datasets that can be included in articles or other publications
- assistance with file conversion for preservation and long-term reuse
- assistance with organizing and documenting complex file structures and project data
- assistance with generating contextual or disciplinary metadata

If you wish to take advantage of these services, please contact data services at ytechdata@vt.edu.

Access Policy

The general intent of VTechData is to make data and other research products openly available to the general public; however, we recognize that certain research situations necessitate restricting access to content for a certain period of time. Restricted objects can be deposited in VTechData if they can, within a well-defined and reasonably short period of time, be made openly accessible to the general public via de-identification or anonymization processes. For assistance, please contact data services at ytechdata@vt.edu.

Restricted objects will be discoverable but not accessible under the terms of deposit. Do not deposit sensitive or confidential data in VTechData; while we make every effort to maintain the privacy of restricted data, any server can be vulnerable. Sensitive data should not be stored online. If you have questions, please contact us.

Deposit Policy

By depositing data or other research materials into VT's Data Repository, you affirm that:
- the deposit represents your own work or the work of your collaborators; any work that is not your own must be properly cited.

Please read our Deposit Agreement before depositing your work.

Members of the Virginia Tech community own copyright in their scholarly or educational works as described in VT Policy 13000 and VT Policy 13015. Copyright owners depositing their works in VTechData retain their copyright while granting a non-exclusive license to Virginia Tech's Libraries for access and preservation purposes. All depositors must agree to the non-exclusive distribution license or place their works in the public domain.

Copyright owners may also elect to license their work via the Creative Commons or Open Data License. This option is available as part of the submission process.

Copyright © 2015 Virginia Polytechnic Institute and State University

Special Collections | Art + Architecture | Veterinary Medicine | Northern Virginia Center Resource Center | Mobile Library Website

VTechData follows Virginia Tech's Privacy Policy

Data Curation Infrastructure

CurateND Data Curation Infrastructure

CurateND uses a Hydra-based discovery application. It uses Fedora Commons 3.x as the object registry and metadata store and Apache Solr as an index. Using both Fedora and Solr is common for Hydra applications. Self-deposit items go through the Hydra application. There is also a batch ingest ability, which deposits items directly into the preservation store as well as Fedora. Objects in Fedora contain pointers to our preservation store. The preservation store is a custom application that puts content into BagIt bags for storage on tape; maintains a disk cache of content; provides a URL for each preserved file; and runs fixity checks on the content. The data is ultimately all stored on tape, with two copies kept locally and two remotely. The tape appliance handles the replication.

Digital Librarians can deal with the batch ingest directly via a networked filesystem. Content is staged on the filesystem, where it can also be reviewed, assessed, and described. When it is ready, the librarian can start an ingest, which copies the data into the preservation system, the metadata into the preservation system, and a copy of the metadata into Fedora. It then asks the Hydra application to index the new content.

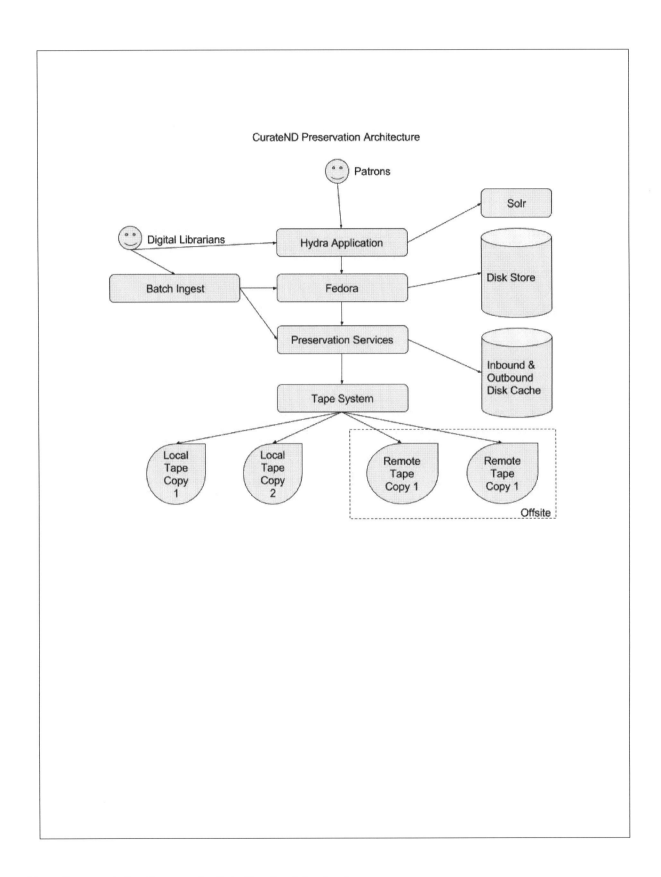

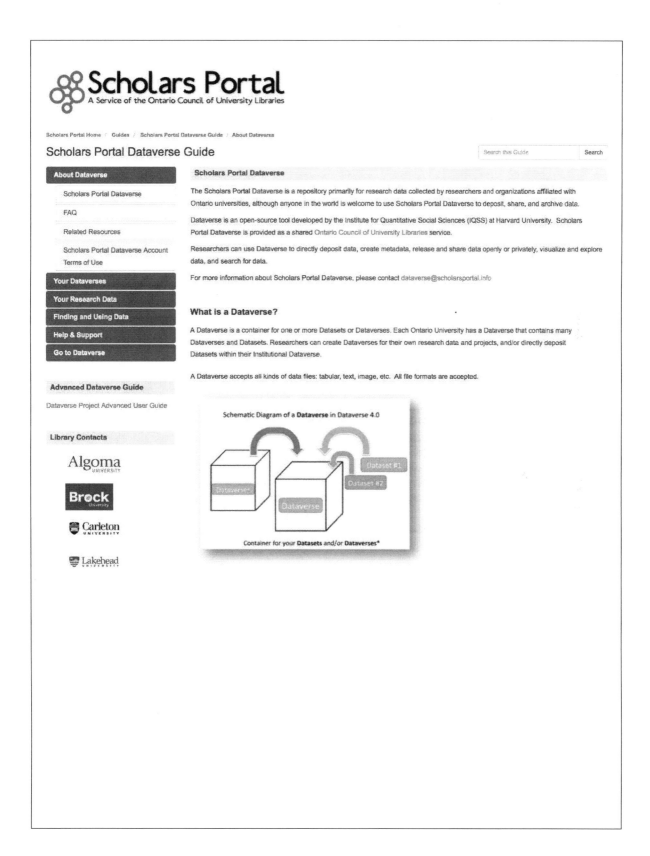

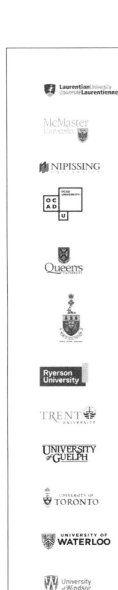

What is a Dataset?

A Dataset is a container for a particular research data set (this can include research data, code, and documentation).

Datasets have an associated metadata record (also referred to as cataloging information or data documentation). This metadata provides contextual information on the dataset. Please see here for more information on creating metadata for datasets.

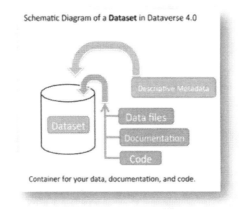

Schematic Diagram of a **Dataset** in Dataverse 4.0

Container for your data, documentation, and code.

Why use Dataverse?

Some key benefits to using Dataverse to manage your research data include:

- **Secure data management**. Dataverse supports the creation of terms of use and restrictions if you want to limit the use of or access to data. It also provides a backup copy for safekeeping.
- **Effective sharing**. Dataverse is a convenient way to disseminate your data, and can facilitate your research team's collaboration within a secure space.
- **Track changes**. Dataverse provides increased control over managing changes to a project without overwriting any part of that project, an especially useful feature when working on a team.
- **Long-term access and preservation**. Persistent identification to your data ensures reliable protection and prevention from data obsolescence.
- **Organization and compatibility**. Create your own personal web data archive that conforms to metadata standards to maximize system compatibility and searchability.
- **Save time**. Dataverse has an easy to use interface for uploading and searching through your data.
- **Increase research visibility**. Increase scholarly recognition for your work beyond your research publications.
- **Meet grant requirements**. Many funding agencies now *require* that researchers deposit data which collected as part of their research project into an archive.

References

Crosas M. The Dataverse Network: An Open-source Application for Sharing, Discovering and Preserving Data. D-Lib Magazine. 2011;Volume 17(1/2).

King, Gary. 2007. An Introduction to the Dataverse Network as an Infrastructure for Data Sharing. Sociological Methods and Research 36: 173–199. Available at http://j.mp/IHJcAa

Data Curation Workflows

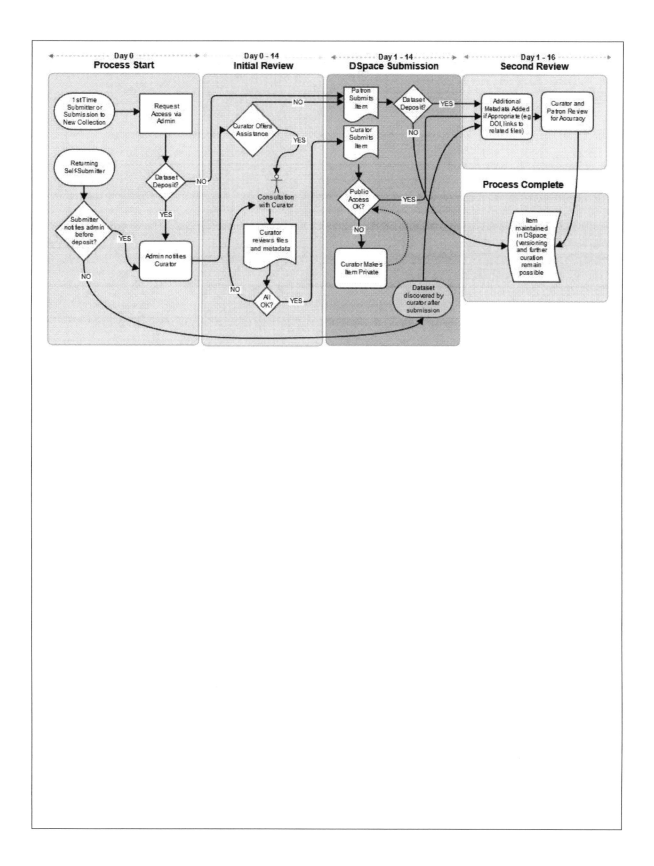

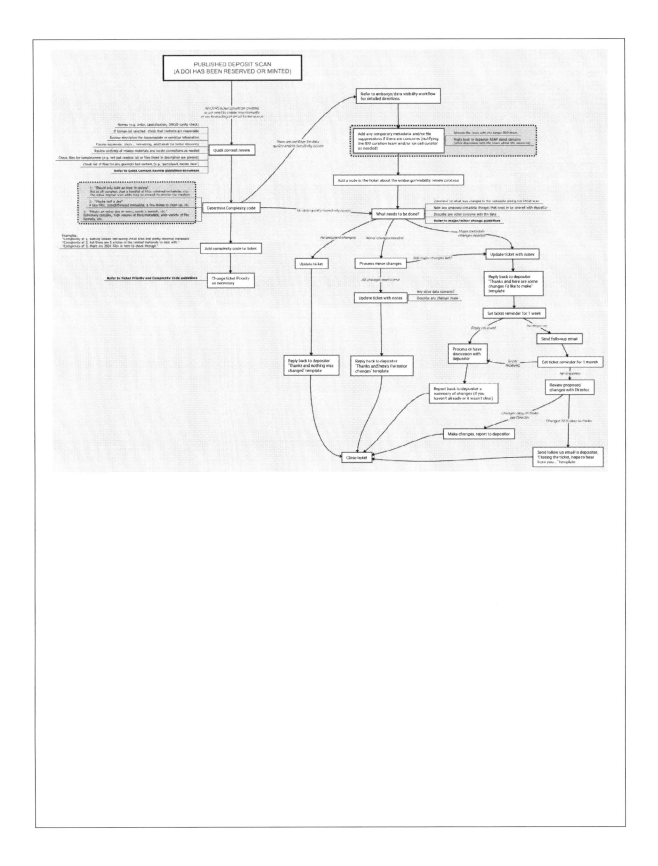

UNIVERSITY OF MINNESOTA LIBRARIES
Curation Workflow (DRUM)
https://drive.google.com/file/d/0B5Dm3XFQloc4d0Q0Nk5lSW92TGs/view?usp=sharing

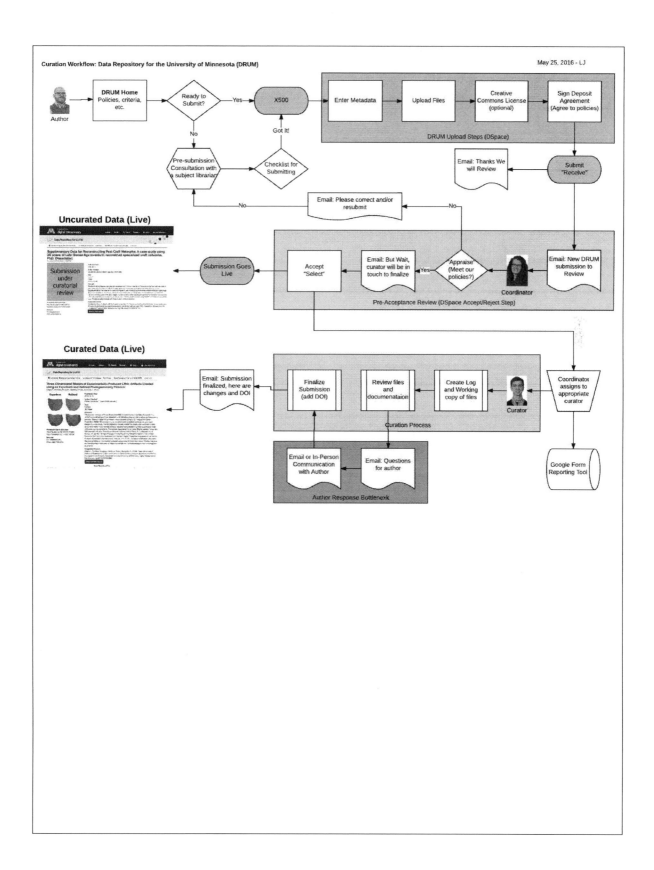

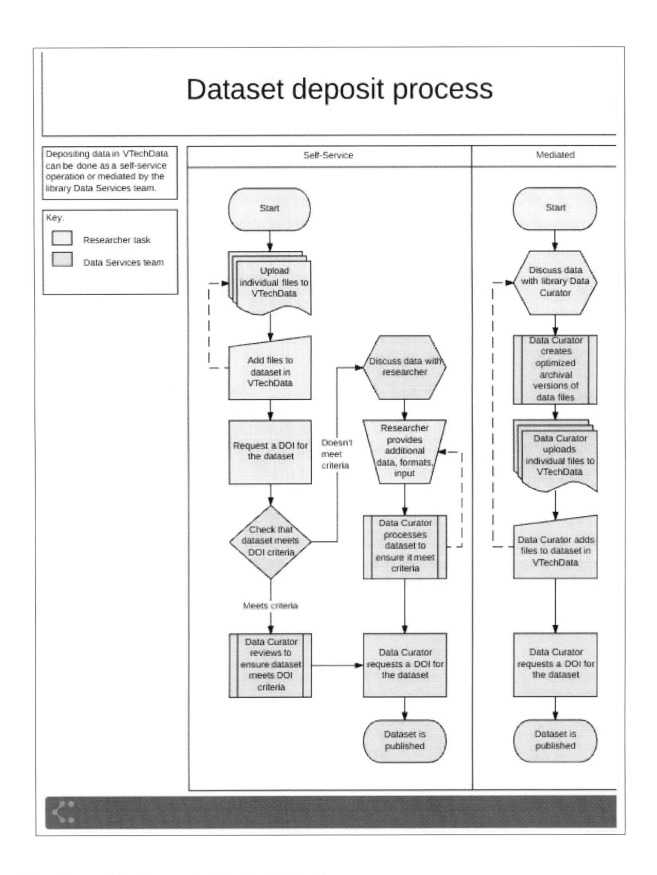

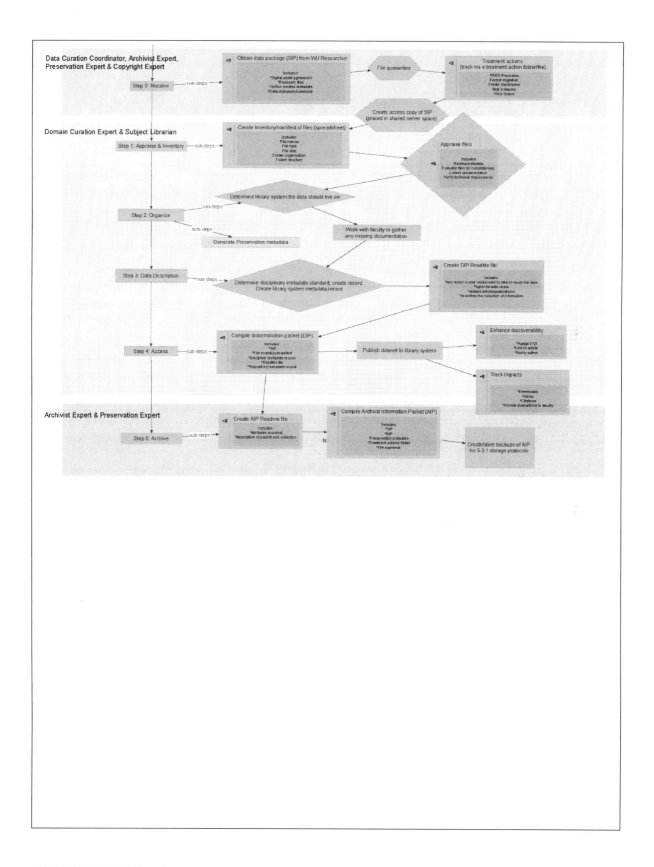

Data Models and Metadata Schemas

CurateND Data Model

Structural Relationships

CurateND uses an early version of the PCDM for structural relationships and a Dublin Core with extensions for the descriptive metadata. Objects have one of three types: LibraryCollection, Work, or Generic File. In practice, while there is a single type of *LibraryCollection* and *GenericFile*, there are many types of *Works*.

All the predicates are in the Fedora Commons 3 external relation namespace, i.e. `info:fedora/fedora-system:def/relations-external#`.

Descriptive Metadata

The descriptive metadata is based on Dublin Core, but has freely added extensions when needed.

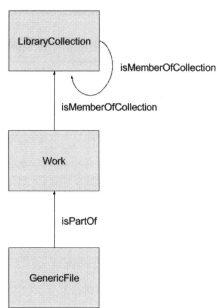

Predicate	Display label	Content Type	Input description	Cardinality (Y=many, N=one)
http://purl.org/dc/terms/alternative	Alternative Title	String, title alternative form.	Already in input page but not displaying?	many
http://purl.org/dc/terms/contributor(unqualified)	Contributor	String, generally personal name. e.g. "Butler, Octavia"	This is also in the input page, but not displaying for books.	many
http://purl.org/dc/terms/contributor#artist	Contributing Artist	String, generally personal name. e.g. "Butler, Octavia"	An entity responsible for creating artistic works within the resource, other than illustrations.	many
http://purl.org/dc/terms/contributor#author	Coauthor	String, generally personal name. e.g. "Butler, Octavia"	An authorial entity who contributed to the resource.	many
http://purl.org/dc/terms/contributor#editor	Contributing Editor	String, generally personal name. e.g. "Butler, Octavia"	An entity responsible for editing the resource.	many
http://purl.org/dc/terms/contributor#illustrator	Contributing Illustrator	String, generally personal name. e.g. "Butler, Octavia"	An entity responsible for illustrating the resource.	many
http://purl.org/dc/terms/contributor#photographer	Contributing Photographer	String, generally personal name. e.g. "Butler, Octavia"	An entity responsible for creating photographic works within the resource.	many
http://purl.org/dc/terms/creator	Inventor	String, generally personal name. e.g. "Butler, Octavia"	An entity listed on the patent as a creator.	Y
http://purl.org/dc/terms/creator (unqualified)	Creator	String, generally personal name. e.g. "Butler, Octavia"	An entity responsible for the resource's creation.	many

http://purl.org/dc/terms/creator #adminstrative_unit	Department	String	Relevant academic departments	Y
http://purl.org/dc/terms/creator #artist	Artist	String, generally personal name. e.g. "Butler, Octavia"	An entity responsible for art works in a resource which consists primarily of art works (e.g. an art book).	many
http://purl.org/dc/terms/creator #author	Author	String, generally personal name. e.g. "Butler, Octavia"	An entity responsible for significant authorial work within the resource.	many
http://purl.org/dc/terms/creator #editor	Editor	String, generally personal name. e.g. "Butler, Octavia"	An entity responsible for significant editorial work in creating the resource.	many
http://purl.org/dc/terms/creator #illustrator	Illustrator	String, generally personal name. e.g. "Butler, Octavia"	An entity responsible for illustrations of a resource which consists primarily of illustrations (e.g. a children's picture book).	many
http://purl.org/dc/terms/creator #local	n/a	String, generally personal name. e.g. "Butler, Octavia"	Creators who are (or were) associated with the local institution. People are to be listed here in addition to being listed in dc:creator.	Y
http://purl.org/dc/terms/creator #photographer	Photographer	String, generally personal name. e.g. "Butler, Octavia"	An entity responsible for photography in a resource which consists primarily of photographs, (e.g. a collection of a photographer's work).	many
http://purl.org/dc/terms/date#a pplication	Application Date	String. (date?) Has form "YYYY-MM-DD"	The date of the initial submission of the application for this patent.	N
http://purl.org/dc/terms/date#pr ior_publication	Prior Publication Date	String. (date?) Has form "YYYY-MM-DD"	Date of prior publication (?)	N
http://purl.org/dc/terms/dateCo pyrighted	Copyright Date	Should be in form YYYY. More granular dates unlikely	The resource's copyright date	one
http://purl.org/dc/terms/datesub mitted	Date Added	Date	Date object was created in CurateND	N

http://purl.org/dc/terms/description	Description	String.	Description of patent, may contain abstract.	Y
http://purl.org/dc/terms/description#table of contents	Table of Contents	String. May be chapter titles separated by a space, two hyphens, and a space, e.g." -- ". Does not need to be parsed specially, can simply be displayed as a string.	A listing of the chapters or sections of a resource as taken from the resource's contents listing.	one
http://purl.org/dc/terms/extent	Extent	String. Will probably be page length, e.g. "368 pages"	The number of pages in the resource, the resource's size, or the resource's duration	many
http://purl.org/dc/terms/extent#claims	Claims	String.	The number of claims in this patent. Usually an integer, but has type string to handle any possible special cases.	N
http://purl.org/dc/terms/identifier#isbn	ISBN	Structured alphanumeric string (regex test: [0-9x]), either 10 or 13 characters. They often contain hyphens, but can be normalized to not.	The resource's ISBN.	many
http://purl.org/dc/terms/identifier#local	Local Identifier	String. For most digitized books, will be the call number, but may be another kind of local identifier used to shelve or handle books.	The resource's local identifier, e.g. call number.	many
http://purl.org/dc/terms/identifier#other application	Other Application	String.	A prior submittal of this patent for review. (?)	Y
http://purl.org/dc/terms/identifier#patent	Patent Number	String. May contains spaces. E.g. "US 1234567890123 B2"	The patent number for this resource. Probably refers to the USPTO but not restricted to US patents.	N

http://purl.org/dc/terms/identifier#prior_publication	Prior Publication Number	String.	Identifier for the prior publication of this patent.	Y
http://purl.org/dc/terms/isPartOf	Published in	String (unfortunately)	The title of the journal, book, or other work in which the Article was published	N
http://purl.org/dc/terms/issued	Publication Date	Should be in form YYYY. More granular dates unlikely	The resource's publication date	one
http://purl.org/dc/terms/issued	Publication Date	Can we test as YYYY or YYYY-MM or YYYY-MM-DD	The article's publication date as year, year-month, or year-month-day, eg. 2015 or 2015-05 or 2015-05-31	N
http://purl.org/dc/terms/issued	Date Issued	String. (See date discussion above)	Date the patent was issued.	N
http://purl.org/dc/terms/isVersionOf#edition	Edition	String. Will probably be a number and additional text: 2, 2ndedition, etc.	The resource's edition.	one
http://purl.org/dc/terms/language	Language	String		Y
http://purl.org/dc/terms/modified	Date Modified	Date	Date object was last modified in CurateND	N
http://purl.org/dc/terms/publisher	Publisher	String		Y
http://purl.org/dc/terms/rights	Rights	String	Intellectual Rights	Y
http://purl.org/dc/terms/rightsHolder	Assignee	String	Assignee of the patent.	Y
http://purl.org/dc/terms/source	USPTO Link	URL.	Link to the patent at the USPTO website (or other patent office websites).	N
http://purl.org/dc/terms/subject#cpc	Classification (CPC)	String.	Cooperative Patent Classification codes.	Y

http://purl.org/dc/terms/subject #ipc	Classification (IPC)	String.	International Patent Classification codes.	Y
http://purl.org/dc/terms/subject #lcsh	Subject (Library of Congress)	String. Taken from the book's bib record. E.g. "Amnesia -- Fiction."	A topic of the content of the resource as taken from the Library of Congress Subject Headings.	many
http://purl.org/dc/terms/subject #uspc	Classification (US Patent)	String.	US Patent Classification codes.	Y
http://purl.org/dc/terms/title	Title	String	Title of the Patent	N
http://purl.org/dc/terms/type	n/a	String	The subtype of Work this item is.	N
http://purl.org/ontology/bibo/eIs sn	e-ISSN	e-ISSN validation?	The e-ISSN of the publication in which the article appears	N
http://purl.org/ontology/bibo/isb n	ISBN	ISBN validation from Book Type?	If the article is published in a volume with an ISBN, the volume's ISBN	N
http://purl.org/ontology/bibo/iss n	ISSN	ISSN validation?	The ISSN of the publication in which the article appears	N
http://purl.org/ontology/bibo/iss ue	Issue	String	The number(s) or name of the issue in which the article appears.	N
http://purl.org/ontology/bibo/nu mPages	Number of pages	Integer	The total number of pages as an integer	N
http://purl.org/ontology/bibo/pa geEnd	Last page	String	The number or other identifier of the article's final page.	N
http://purl.org/ontology/bibo/pa geStart	First page	String	The number or other identifier of the first page on which the article appears, e.g. "42" or "E594"	N
http://purl.org/ontology/bibo/vol ume	Volume	String	The number or name of the volume in which the article appears.	N

QUICK START GUIDE: SIMPLE CREATE

Using EZID's UI, you can quickly and easily create ARKs and DOIs. If you do not know any of the values for the properties outlined below, see the Quick Start Guide "What to do if required information is unavailable.

FOR ARKS

Property	Description	Examples
Object location URL	The current location (URL) of the identified object.	http://merritt.cdlib.org/m/ark%3A%2F13030%2Fqt5np807ch http://opencontext.org/subjects/199ED3F0-8CA2-4BBD-FA14-468133255587 http://www.coredu.fr/repository/OAIHandler?verb=GetRecord&metadataPrefix=lom&identifier=oai:editors.coredu.fr:31779
Who	The name of an entity (person, organization, or service) responsible for creating the content or making it available, e.g. author, creator. Put name parts in "sort-friendly" order. Separate multiple names with ";". Append one or more final commas (",") to indicate that one or more internal commas can be used as inversion points to recover natural word order (if different from sort-friendly word order).	Kim, JH,; Cho, J,; Keane, TD, Virginia Department of Historic Resources (VA-DHR); Open Context Editors Canal Educatif à la Demande
What	A name or other human-oriented identifier given to the resource, e.g. a title.	Political fragmentation and land use changes in the Interior Plains Virginia Site Files: 44WR0079 (Site) Vidéos Sciences & Innovation de Canal Éducatif à la Demande
When	A point or period of time (date range) important in the lifecycle of the resource, often when it was created, modified, or made available. Use ";" to separate entries and "~" to indicate approximation.	10/4/2015 2014-07-31T00:00:00-07:00 1/1/2007

FOR DOIs

Property	Description	Examples
Object location URL	The current location (URL) of the identified object.	https://lilliput.figshare.com/articles/Impact_of_Task_Performance_Fraud_Risk_Assessment_on_Forensic_Skills_and_Mindsets_Experience_from_Nigeria/2002749 http://doi.virtualbrain.org/lp/10.5072/FK2028TW8Z http://mdsoarstage.lib.umd.edu/handle/11603-STAGE/4859
Creator	The main researchers involved in producing the data, or the authors of the publication in priority order. May be a corporate, institutional, or personal name. In personal names, list family name before given name.	George, Christopher Worth, A [MGH] Owens, Allessia P.
Title	A name or title by which the data or publication is known.	Impact of Task Performance Fraud Risk Assessment on Forensic Skills and Mindsets: Experience from Nigeria Internet Brain Segmentation Repository Mentoring African American males
Publisher	A holder of the data (e.g., an archive) or the institution which submitted the work. In the case of datasets, the publisher is the entity primarily responsible for making the data available to the research community.	Figshare MGH CMA Maryland Shared Open Access Repository
Publication year	The year when the data was or will be made publicly available. If an embargo period is in effect, use the year when the embargo period ends.	2015 2015 2008
Resource type	The general type of the data.	Dataset Dataset Text

QUICK START GUIDE: ADVANCED CREATE FOR DOIs

Using EZID's UI to create a DOI, you must provide DataCite metadata.
Mandatory DataCite properties are indicated with an asterisk (*).

Property	Description	Notes
Creator* (repeats)	The main researchers involved in producing the data, or the authors of the publication, in priority order. Mandatory	Personal, corporate, or institutional name(s)
Title* (repeats)	A name or title by which a resource is known. Mandatory	Free text
Publisher*	The name of the entity that holds, archives, publishes, prints, distributes, releases, issues, or produces the resource. Mandatory	Free text
PublicationYear*	The year when the data was or will be made publicly available. Mandatory	YYYY
ResourceType	A description of the resource. Uses a controlled vocabulary. Recommended, but *will become mandatory in next version.*	See Quick Start Guide for controlled list
Subject (repeats)	Subject, keyword, classification code, or key phrase describing the resource. Recommended	Free text
Contributor (repeats)	The institution or person responsible for collecting, managing, distributing, or otherwise contributing to the development of the resource. Recommended	See Quick Start Guide for controlled list. Works with ORCIDs.
Date (repeats)	Different dates relevant to the work. Recommended	Uses W3CDTF formats
Language	The primary language of the resource. Optional	Allowed values are taken from IETF BCP 47, ISO 639-1 language codes
AlternateIdentifier (repeats)	An identifier or identifiers other than the primary Identifier applied to the resource being registered. Optional	Free text
RelatedIdentifier (repeats)	Identifiers of related resources. (Must be globally unique.) Recommended	See Quick Start Guide for controlled list
Size (repeats)	Unstructured size information about the resource. Optional	Free text
Format (repeats)	Technical format of the resource. Optional	Free text
Version	The version number of the resource. Suggested practice: track major_version.minor_version. Optional	Free text
Rights (repeats)	Any rights information for this resource. Optional	Free text
Description (repeats)	All additional information that does not fit in any of the other categories. May be used for technical information. Recommended	Abstract strongly suggested
GeoLocation (with point and box sub-properties)	Spatial region or named place where the data was gathered or about which the data is focused. Recommended	Can use WGS 84 (World Geodetic System) coordinates or free text

For details about field constraints and all sub-properties, see http://schema.datacite.org

Data Deaccessioning Policies

Illinois Data Bank   + Deposit Dataset   Q Find Data   ⓘ Policies   ❓ Help   Log In with NetID

Policy Framework and Definitions
Access and Use Policy
Accession Policy
Deposit Agreement
Preservation Policy
Preservation Review Procedures
Withdrawal Guidelines
Preservation Review Guidelines

Preservation Review, Retention, Deaccession, Revision, and Withdrawal Procedure

Purpose of this Procedure

This document outlines the procedures for reviewing, revising, retaining, Deaccessioning, and Withdrawing Data Files, Metadata Files, and Descriptive Metadata published in the Illinois Data Bank.

Preservation Review

The long-term viability of Datasets published in the Illinois Data Bank will be assessed using a robust set of review criteria. The Illinois Data Bank is committed to transparency, accountability, and collaborative decision-making regarding assessments of the long-term preservation status of research data. While a variety of unique factors influence decisions made about the Disposition of Datasets, the criteria outlined in the Preservation Review Guidelines provide a basis for assessing Datasets.

Preservation Review Roles and Responsibilities

Assessment decisions are a shared responsibility and are often influenced by discipline-specific factors. The Research Data Service staff are responsible for developing and leading the assessment process of Datasets and will consult with ad hoc "Assessment Teams" comprising functional and subject specialists as well as domain experts outside of the Library as appropriate. The "Assessment Team" may also incorporate input from other stakeholders as necessary.

Retention

The Illinois Data Bank anticipates that the majority of Preservation Reviews will result in Dataset retention. The decision to retain a Dataset will typically indicate that the preservation viability of the Dataset is acceptable given the determined long-term value of the Dataset, and that Illinois Data Bank resources being deployed to steward the Dataset are at a level that is proportional to its long-term value.

The Illinois Data Bank will commit resources to escalating preservation efforts for Datasets determined to have remarkable value that are suffering preservation risk or are not available in the most usable states. Examples of escalated preservation procedures include file format migration, enhancing Descriptive Metadata/Metadata Files, or improving access and/or use services by developing data-type-specific viewers/emulators.

Deaccession

A decision to Deaccession the Data Files and/or Metadata Files associated with a Dataset will only occur if it is determined that the Dataset is not of long-term value to its research community and/or its inclusion in the Illinois Data Bank detrimentally affects the Illinois Data Bank's ability to steward effectively other resources whose research value and preservation viability are evident.

Upon deciding to Deaccession the Data Files and/or Metadata Files associated with a Dataset, the Illinois Data Bank will consider one of these options:

- Transfer to a repository more appropriately situated to steward the Data Files and/or Metadata Files.
- Transfer Data Files and/or Metadata Files back to the Long-Term Contact Person indicated in the Descriptive Metadata.

For any Data Files and/or Metadata Files that are to be Deaccessioned, a good faith effort to contact the Long-Term Contact Person will be made by notifying them at the email address the Illinois Data Bank has on record. The notification will outline the Illinois Data Bank's Deaccessioning decision.

If the Illinois Data Bank does not receive a response from the Long-Term Contact Person after 90 days, the Illinois Data Bank will transfer or discard the Data Files and/or Metadata Files according to the practices and security standards in place at the time of Deaccessioning.

The Illinois Data Bank will not Deaccession any Data Files and/or Metadata Files before the initial commitment period ends, currently five years.

The Illinois Data Bank currently plans to retain Descriptive Metadata persistently for all Datasets deposited in the Illinois Data Bank regardless of the Disposition of Data File(s) and/or Metadata File(s) except in rare circumstances as determined by the Director of the Research Data Service.

Illinois Data Bank   + Deposit Dataset   Q Find Data   ⓘ Policies   ❓ Help   Log in with NetID

Policy Framework and Definitions

Access and Use Policy

Accession Policy

Deposit Agreement

Preservation Policy

Preservation Review Procedures

Withdrawal Guidelines

Preservation Review Guidelines

Revisions

Depositors are expected to confirm the validity of all content prior to publishing a Dataset. However, should an error in the Descriptive Metadata be discovered, the original Depositor or Research Data Service staff may make a revision to the Descriptive Metadata, which is tracked via a public change log.

If a Creator of a Dataset finds that a file in their published Dataset contains an error, they must contact the Research Data Service staff to submit the corrected file. A new version of the entire Dataset will be created and a new DOI will be assigned. Research Data Service staff will see that the Descriptive Metadata associated with the Dataset makes apparent which version is most recent and what changes occurred. Research Data Service staff will refer to the Illinois Data Bank Withdrawal Guidelines when determining whether to remove the erroneous Dataset from public view. Depositors are expected to limit the need for versioning by not publishing erroneous Datasets; as such, Datasets are limited to no more than six versions.

Withdrawal of Deposited Datasets

The Illinois Data Bank may Withdraw a published Dataset from the repository before the current five year commitment period ends for a compelling reason. Compelling reasons include, but are not limited to, failure to meet the Criteria for Depositing outlined in the Illinois Data Bank Accession Policy, detection of malware in deposited files, violations of copyright or publisher policy, violations of contracts (e.g., Nondisclosure Agreement, Material Transfer Agreement, etc.), research misconduct (e.g., plagiarism, fabrication or falsification of data, etc.), legal requirements, national security, or situations that violate the University Code of Conduct.

Datasets may not be Withdrawn because the Depositor or Creator is moving to another institution. Creators have the right to provide additional copies to other institutions under the non-exclusive Deposit Agreement.

All Withdrawal requests must be submitted to databank@library.illinois.edu. These will be reviewed by Research Data Service staff who may contact the requestor for more information. If the request is submitted by a third party or the decision to Withdraw is made by the Research Data Service staff, the Long-Term Contact Person and the Depositor will be notified of the request via the email addresses the Illinois Data Bank has on record. Research Data Service staff are not responsible for resolving legal disputes, but will refer University of Illinois community members to the University of Illinois Office of University Counsel at http://www.legal.uillinois.edu/.

At minimum, Data Files and/or Metadata Files associated with a Withdrawn Dataset are removed from the public view and are no longer available for download. Research Data Service staff will add a statement of Withdrawal to the associated Dataset's Descriptive Metadata. In many cases, Withdrawal results in suppression of public access to Data Files and/or Metadata Files, even when the entire Dataset will be retained within our systems for the sake of provenance. In rarer cases, the Research Data Service staff may be compelled to delete all or part of a Dataset altogether. The Research Data Service staff will refer to the Illinois Data Bank Withdrawal Guidelines to respond to the varying circumstances under which Withdrawal may occur.

Withdrawal of Dataset Drafts

In order to ensure sustainability of technological and storage resources, the Research Data Service staff retain the right to delete initiated Datasets that have remained in draft state in the Illinois Data Bank in excess of 12 months. A good faith effort to contact the Depositor via the email address on record in the Illinois Data Bank will be made prior to deletion.

Acknowledgements

- Carnegie Mellon University Research Showcase. Research Showcase @ CMU Policies, Revision and Withdrawal Policy. http://repository.cmu.edu/policies.html
- Illinois Digital Environment for Access to Learning and Scholarship (IDEALS). IDEALS Withdrawal Policy. http://hdl.handle.net/2142/3744

Contact Research Data Service staff with questions or to request an addition or revision to this policy.

3. Collections & Content

Defining Research Data

For the purposes of Deep Blue Data, research data are defined as representations of observations, objects, or other entities used as evidence of phenomena for the purposes of research or scholarship. In practical terms, Deep Blue Data will accept data that were developed or used in the support of research activities of U-M faculty, students and staff.

Data Formats

As the intent of the Deep Blue Data data repository is to make data as openly available as possible for discovery, understanding, and reuse, we strongly encourage the submission of data in formats that are open and nonproprietary.

If data cannot be converted to nonproprietary formats, we then encourage data submission in formats that are widely used.

Deep Blue Data will accept data in proprietary formats provided that these formats are appropriate for the research communities who are likely to have an interest in the data. However, it may not be possible to provide as high a level of preservation service for proprietary formats (see Preservation Policy).

Retention Review

Data submitted to Deep Blue Data will be reviewed after 10 years to determine if a data set should be retained and be subject to further, periodic, reviews thereafter. The goal of these reviews is to identify and possibly remove data that have reached the end of their use and reuse life cycle, or have become inaccessible (e.g. because of format obsolescence). The retention review will be conducted by the Data Curation Librarian, appropriate subject librarian(s), and, whenever possible, the depositor. The retention decision will be driven by a determination of the ongoing value to the research community. Long-term retention will also be determined by file format based preservation levels assigned upon deposit. Any data removed from the repository will be returned to the depositor whenever possible and documented with a tombstone record, which is the remaining metadata from a deleted record kept for the purposes of permanence.

Removing work from Deep Blue Data

Depositors can remove their work from Deep Blue Data with the assistance of and after consultation with staff if there is a mutual determination that the work is not appropriate for the service. Whenever work is removed, a tombstone record will remain.

If the depositor requests that the data be withdrawn from Deep Blue Data, the Library will take the following factors into consideration:

- If the data has been shown to contain inaccurate or faulty information
- If there is evidence of the data being used, cited, or downloaded

The Library also reserves the right to remove any deposit for reasons including:

- It was not appropriate for deposit (e.g. it contains sensitive information, viruses or other malware, or if we receive a verified complaint that it contains materials determined to be an infringement of copyright)
- It is no longer of active interest as described below (see the Retention Review section)

In such cases we will make reasonable attempts to contact the depositor so they can arrange for a new home for the data. A tombstone record will always remain for any deposit that is removed.

Copyright and Take-Down Notification

Please refer to the library and University policy and procedures on copyright and take-down.

https://www.dropbox.com/sh/jbo7eovk5q06bv8vjdi0f6xfk7KFA/sampling.doc

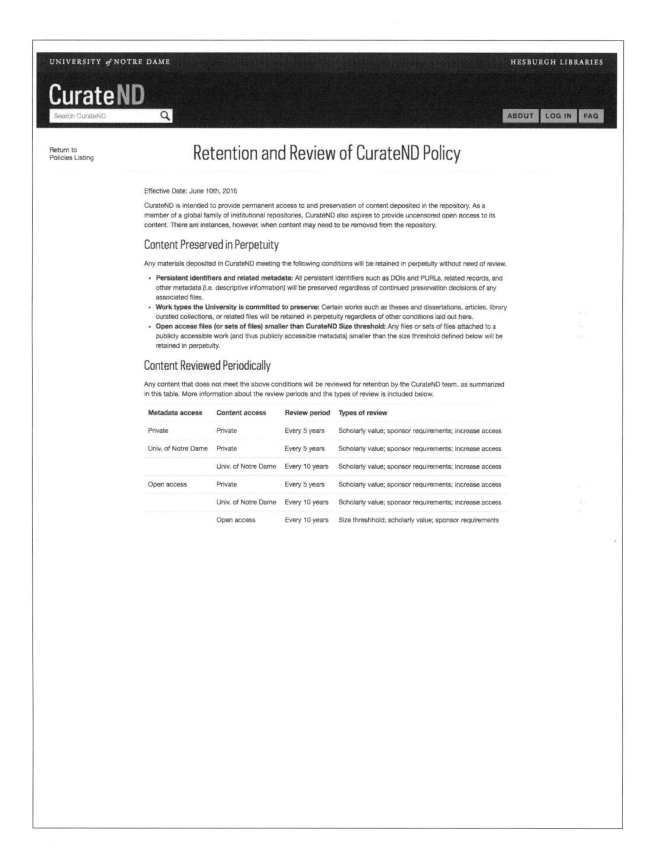

Review Periods

Content (and associated metadata) not retained in perpetuity will be reviewed every 5 or 10 years, as indicated above. The clock starts from the year that the content was deposited. For example, if private content with private metadata is deposited in CurateND in 2017, it will be reviewed in 2022, 5 years after depositing.

Types of Review

Scholarly Value Determination

In consultation with the content owner, if possible, a library subject specialist, related campus department, or other domain expert will make a determination for continued retention. If none of these individuals or groups can be contacted or make a determination, the University Committee on Libraries (UCL) will be consulted. The determination to continue preservation will be made based on at least the following criteria:

- Have past usage rates via CurateND been high or low?
- Is content likely to be used, or continue to be used in the future (i.e., has the content been superseded by other scholarship)?
- Is the content deemed especially rare, ephemeral, unique, or significant?

Please note: Any work with metadata marked private (and thus with private content) may be removed if further preservation requirements are not documented or cannot be proven by content owners.
Also note: CurateND will make reasonable efforts to contact content owners based on available information. If content owners cannot be reached, the Hesburgh Libraries will make the final determination as to whether content should continue to be preserved.

Size Threshold

CurateND will maintain a size threshold for a single file. Currently, this size threshold is 50 GB. This size threshold itself will be periodically reviewed and extended based on technological advancements.

Research Sponsor Retention Requirements

If research funding or other project requirements deem that content needs to be preserved for a specified amount of time, the CurateND team will do so depending on the resource support needed for that content.

Please note: If the content has preservation requirements, but does not meet the scholarly value determination, exceeds the current size threshold, and was deposited more than 10 years ago, the CurateND team may seek compensation from the content owner in order to continue preserving the content.

Increase Access

For all content reviewed that is not open access (it is assumed open access content will also have open access metadata), the content owner or proxy will be asked to increase access to at least the next level, if copyright or other circumstances allow. For example, can private metadata be made accessible to the University of Notre Dame? Or if content is accessible to the University, can it be made open access?

 Texas Data Repository

VII. Deaccessioning Data

Items may be deaccessioned from the repository for the following reasons:

- copyright violation
- legal requirements and proven violations
- national security
- falsified research
- confidentiality concerns etc.

Items may also be deaccessioned from the repository by the depositor. Deaccessioning a dataset or a version of a dataset is a very serious action that should only occur if there is a legal or valid reason for the dataset to no longer be accessible to the public. If you absolutely must deaccession, you can deaccession a version of a dataset or an entire dataset. To deaccession, go to a dataset you've already published (or add a new one and publish it), click on Edit Dataset, then Deaccession Dataset. If you have multiple versions of a dataset, you can select here which versions you want to deaccession or choose to deaccession the entire dataset. You must also include a reason as to why this dataset was deaccessioned from a dropdown list of options. There is also a free-text box to add more details as to why this was deaccessioned. If the dataset has moved to a different repository or site you are encouraged to include a URL (preferably persistent) for users to continue to be able to access this dataset in the future.

Important Note: A tombstone landing page with the basic citation metadata will always be accessible to the public if they use the persistent URL (Handle or DOI) provided in the citation for that dataset. Users will not be able to see any of the files or additional metadata that were previously available prior to deaccession.

Should a dataset be removed by either the repository or the depositor, TDL reserves the right to retain its citation metadata record in the repository as trace of the dataset. Additionally, the citation metadata of withdrawn items will be searchable.

References

DISC-UK DataShare Project, "Policy-making for Research Data in Repositories: A Guide," https://www.coar-repositories.org/files/guide.pdf

Dataverse Project, "User Guide: Dataset + File Management," http://guides.dataverse.org/en/latest/user/dataset-management.html

Footnotes

1. These General Terms of Use are adapted from Harvard Dataverse generic best practices templates created for these purposes. For original, see: http://best-practices.Dataverse.org/harvard-policies/harvard-terms-of-use.html)
2. The Privacy Policy is adapted from Harvard Dataverse best practices generic templates created for these purposes. For the original, please see: http://best-practices.Dataverse.org/harvard-policies/harvard-privacy-policy.html
3. Adapted from https://creativecommons.org/publicdomain/zero/1.0/
4. Adapted from the Data Citation Synthesis Group, "Joint Declaration of Data Citation Principles": https://www.force11.org/group/joint-declaration-data-citation-principles-final
5. The Texas Data Repository Community Norms are adapted from Harvard Dataverse best practices templates created for these purposes. For original templates, please see http://best-practices.Dataverse.org/harvard-policies/community-norms.html. Important modifications to this section include more extensive use of the Joint Declaration of Data Citation Principles.
6. Adapted from Data Citation Synthesis Group: Joint Declaration of Data Citation Principles. Martone M. (ed.) San Diego CA: FORCE11; 2014 [/datacitation].
7. The Data Usage Agreement is adapted from the Harvard best practices templates created for these purposes. For original template, please see http://best-practices.Dataverse.org/harvard-policies/sample-dua.html

Data Curation Job Descriptions

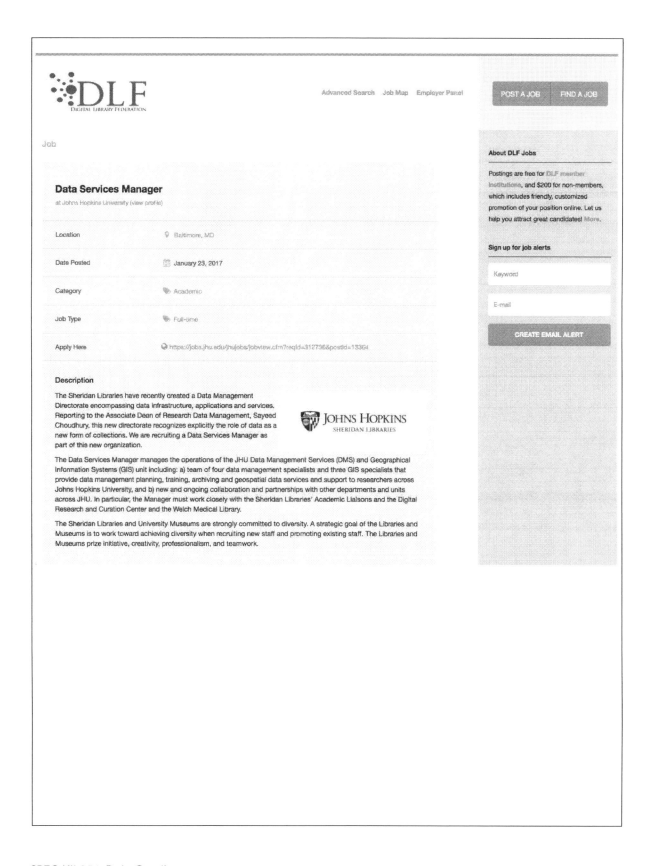

Data Services Manager

at Johns Hopkins University (view profile)

Location	⚲ Baltimore, MD
Date Posted	🗓 January 23, 2017
Category	🏷 Academic
Job Type	🏷 Full-time
Apply Here	⚲ https://jobs.jhu.edu/jhujobs/jobview.cfm?reqId=312736&pcetId=13364

Description

The Sheridan Libraries have recently created a Data Management Directorate encompassing data infrastructure, applications and services. Reporting to the Associate Dean of Research Data Management, Sayeed Choudhury, this new directorate recognizes explicitly the role of data as a new form of collections. We are recruiting a Data Services Manager as part of this new organization.

The Data Services Manager manages the operations of the JHU Data Management Services (DMS) and Geographical Information Systems (GIS) unit including: a) team of four data management specialists and three GIS specialists that provide data management planning, training, archiving and geospatial data services and support to researchers across Johns Hopkins University, and b) new and ongoing collaboration and partnerships with other departments and units across JHU. In particular, the Manager must work closely with the Sheridan Libraries' Academic Liaisons and the Digital Research and Curation Center and the Welch Medical Library.

The Sheridan Libraries and University Museums are strongly committed to diversity. A strategic goal of the Libraries and Museums is to work toward achieving diversity when recruiting new staff and promoting existing staff. The Libraries and Museums prize initiative, creativity, professionalism, and teamwork.

University of Michigan Library

POSITION DESCRIPTION

Job Description

The Research Data Curation Librarian will advance the library's mission to create and sustain data services for the campus that support the mission of the University of Michigan researchers through the library's Research Data Services (RDS) unit. A key focus of this position will be to contribute to the development of the data repository in collaboration with colleagues and stakeholders, in the library and across campus.

Date: 8/2015
Department: Science, Engineering, Clark Library and Research Data Services
Working Title: Research Data Curation Librarian
University Classification: <Librarian>

Position Summary:

The University of Michigan Library has embarked on an aggressive and exciting initiative to address research data management and curation needs at the University.

RDS is responsible for strategic planning, coordination, and deployment of research data services directed at facilitating the research lifecycle. This includes creating and implementing data management assistance for the campus, outreach to faculty in collaboration with librarian subject specialists, informationists, training, and assessment of RDS programs and services. RDS operates in 4 key areas: 1) Education, Awareness and Community Building, 2) Technical Infrastructure, 3) Policy and Strategy, and 4) Consultation and Services.

The responsibilities of the Research Data Curation Librarian will fall in all four of the above areas, with a particular focus on developing and maintaining the services offered through the research data repository in collaboration with colleagues and stakeholders, in the library and across campus.

Reporting Structure:
Reports to the Research Data Services Manager

Supervisory Experience:
This is a largely collaborative position that requires negotiation of relationships across the library

and the University. As such, it will require student supervision and deployment experience, but has no FTEs reporting to it.

Responsibilities (essential functions):

While partnering with colleagues at the U-M Office of Research, Information Technology Services, Advanced Research Computing, as well as academic programs, institutes, departments, and colleges across campus, the Research Data Curation Librarian will:

Work with researchers to curate and archive data (30%)
The Librarian will work with researchers to identify, recruit, ingest and deposit data in the library's digital repository, adhering to local policies, national and international standards and best practices. The incumbent will play a significant role in outreach to the research community to deposit data in both the digital repository or an appropriate subject repository, as well as creating training programs, help guides and web resources for Data Education and RDS for internal and external audiences. When necessary the Librarian will consult with researchers on their specific needs such as adopting metadata standards or data sensitivity characterization.

Create, support and sustain technical infrastructure (20%)
In collaboration with key partners, the incumbent will act as the point person for the data repository, investigate integrative infrastructures to connect campus needs to the repository, design and implement workflows, and execute technical processes involved in managing the lifecycle of digital datasets including data transformation projects.

Work with campus stakeholders on larger data collections issues (15%)
In addition to serving as a consultant to researchers and librarians on data issues and services, performs data management planning with principle investigators and researchers; assists in the development and delivery of training and instructional materials on data curation; provides guidance and instruction on discovery, acquisition and use of research data in the public domain.

Engage and participate in all aspects of the RDS and library services as appropriate (25%)
The Research Data Curation Librarian will participate in developing RDS within the Library and actively working to promote and advance the components of RDS amongst librarians. This includes the development of resources, documentation and instructional content about data curation, participating in selected cross-library working groups to create and improve services. Other duties as assigned.

Professional Development (10%)
Pursue research and professional development activities individually and as appropriate to the position. Engage with the library community and communities of practice beyond the library.

Required Qualifications:

- ALA-accredited Master's degree or an equivalent combination of a relevant advanced degree and experience
- Demonstrated knowledge of or direct experience managing and curating research data
- Knowledge of information technologies, standards and best practices prevalent in digital or data curation
- Ability to articulate roles in the research data ecosystem
- Knowledge of technologies for data management and curation, and familiarity with preservation principles and practices
- Ability to work independently and effectively with others as a team within a complex and fluid organization. Ability to work well in a multicultural and collaborative environment
- Possess excellent written and oral communication skills; ability to present and share ideas clearly and effectively to a diverse audience

Desired Qualifications
- Experience working with digital repository or content management systems
- Experience documenting workflows and procedures
- Knowledge of metadata formats, including Dublin Core, MODS, METS, and data exchange protocols such as SWORD and OAI-PMH.
- Experience in identifying researcher information needs and in creating effective services to meet those needs
- Demonstrated experience in the acquisition and management of born-digital or digitized library, archival, or research materials
- Demonstrated time management and project completion skills
- Demonstrated commitment to customer service

Digital Library Data Curation Developer

The Hesburgh Libraries is seeking a passionate software developer to join our Digital Library Technology Unit in support of digital library and research data curation services. With an emphasis on data curation, the individual will design and develop digital library frameworks and applications in areas such as controlled vocabularies, digital collections, digital content harvesting. Within science, engineering, and the social sciences, the individual will work with librarians, campus partners, and researchers to embed research data curation tools and workflows into active research projects for archiving and sharing data in our institutional repository CurateND (http://curate.nd.edu), or other relevant community repositories. This will involve combining data tool and architecture design with development of automated data extraction utilities and linked data technologies to apply domain specific metadata. The individual will also develop web based user clients for researchers to manage and browse research data. Additionally, the individual will contribute to our digital library frameworks and applications in areas such as controlled vocabularies, digital collections, digital content harvesting, and general support of digital library applications.

This position includes the opportunity to join us in a vibrant open source project called Hydra (http://projecthydra.org) in which we have partnered with several other universities and organizations to create advanced digital library applications and services.

Job duties include:

- Design and develop digital library applications supporting digital library and data curation services

- Provide technical leadership in data architecture and design for digital library data projects in collaboration with the Digital Library Technology Unit

- With campus partners, develop services and web clients to manage, archive, and share research data

- Create APIs and processes to integrate other campus systems with CurateND from groups like Engineering Science and Computing, Center for Research Computing, and Digital Production.

- Work with librarians and campus partners through our Center for Digital Scholarship to develop data models and tools to tag and describe data and collections with domain specific ontologies

- Provide software development support for research projects involving computational analysis or scientific data. This may involve manipulating or analyzing data with a statistical/computational package (e.g. R, SciPy, Matlab, Mathematica, STATA)

- Support digital humanities projects as needed with automated text analysis, topic modeling, and other methods

Minimum Qualifications

- Bachelors degree in Computer Science or related discipline, or equivalent software development work experience.

- At least 2 years experience working with at least one programming language (such as Python, Ruby on Rails, C, C++, Java, Python).

- At least 2 years experience creating relational databases using Oracle, MySQL, Postgres, or other modern RDBMS.

- Experience developing web based user interfaces and/or applications

- Experience designing and implementing APIs or middleware related services
- Excellent personal skills in order to work closely with customers throughout the research lifecycle

Preferred Qualifications

- Experience developing against digital repository systems such as Hydra, Islandora, Fedora Commons, or DSpace
- Experience with search indexes such as Solr, Lucene, and ElasticSearch
- Experience with research ontologies, RDF, or other linked data technologies
- Experience developing search, browse, or other visualization interfaces for research data
- Experience with computational and statistical packages such as R, Matlab, SPSS, SAS, and STATA.
- Applied research experience as either a member or in support of a science or engineering research project involving data computation or analysis
- Experience with digital humanities computational techniques such as text mining, or topic modeling

Selected Resources

Data Curation Practices and Treatments (multidisciplinary)

Akers, Katherine Goold. 2013. "Looking Out for the Little Guy: Small Data Curation." *Bulletin of the American Society for Information Science and Technology*. March. http://www.asis.org/Bulletin/Feb-13/FebMar13_RDAP_Akers.pdf.

Duerr, Ruth E, Mark A Parsons, Melinda Marquis, Rudy Dichtl, and Teresa Mullins. 2004. "Challenges in Long-Term Data Stewardship." In *Proc. 21st IEEE Conference on Mass Storage Systems and Technologies*, 47–67. College Park, MD, USA: NASA/CP-2004-212750.

Gold, Anna K. 2010. "Data Curation and Libraries: Short-Term Developments, Long-Term Prospects." https://works.bepress.com/agold01/9/.

Gold, Anna K. 2007. "Cyberinfrastructure, Data, and Libraries, Part 2: Libraries and the Data Challenge: Roles and Actions for Libraries." *D-Lib Magazine* 13 (9/10). http://works.bepress.com/agold01/4/.

Higgins, Sarah. 2008. "The DCC Curation Lifecycle Model." *International Journal of Digital Curation* 3 (1): 134–40. doi:10.2218/ijdc.v3i1.48.

Johnston, Lisa R., ed. 2017. *Curating Research Data, Volume Two: A Handbook of Current Practice*. ACRL. (print) http://www.alastore.ala.org/detail.aspx?ID=11961 (online OA version) http://hdl.handle.net/11299/185335.

Johnston, Lisa R., Jake Carlson, Patricia Hswe, C.R.H. Vitale, Heidi Imker, Wendy Kozlowski, Robert Olendorf, and Claire Stewart. 2017. "Data Curation Network: How Do We Compare? A Snapshot of Six Academic Library Institutions' Data Repository and Curation Services." *Journal of eScience Librarianship* 6 (1). doi:10.7191/jeslib.2017.1102.

Johnston, Lisa R., Jake Carlson, C.R.H. Vitale, Heidi Imker, Wendy Kozlowski, Robert Olendorf, and Claire Stewart. 2017b. "Results of the Fall 2016 Data Curation Pilot through the Data Curation Network." https://docs.google.com/document/d/14Lp734CzZRJgZWYixGg1DMr9WEiWcM0wPBD0SQvcAko/edit?usp=sharing

Johnston, Lisa R. 2014. A Workflow Model for Curating Research Data in the University of Minnesota Libraries: Report from the 2013 Data Curation Pilot. University of Minnesota Digital Conservancy. Retrieved from the University of Minnesota Digital Conservancy, http://hdl.handle.net/11299/162338.

Johnston, Lisa, R., Jake Carlson, C.R.H. Vitale, Heidi Imker, Wendy Kozlowski, Robert Olendorf, and Claire Stewart. 2016. "Definitions of Data Curation Activities." https://drive.google.com/file/d/0B5Dm3XFQloc4Y1RGTmIwM0VyWUE/view?usp=sharing.

Kozlowski, Wendy. 2014. "Guidelines for Writing 'readme' Style Metadata." Research Data Management Services Group, May. http://data.research.cornell.edu/sites/default/files/SciMD_ReadMe_Guidelines_v4_1_0.pdf.

Lee, Dong Joon, and Besiki Stvilia. 2017. "Practices of Research Data Curation in Institutional Repositories: A Qualitative View from Repository Staff." *PLOS ONE* 12 (3): e0173987. doi:10.1371/journal.pone.0173987.

Noonan, Daniel, and Tamar Chute. 2014. "Data Curation and the University Archives." The American Archivist 77 (1): 201–40. http://dx.doi.org/10.17723/aarc.77.1.m49r46526847g587.

Weber, Nicholas M., Andrea K. Thomer, Matthew S. Mayernik, Bob Dattore, Zaihua Ji, and Steve Worley. 2013. "The Product and System Specificities of Measuring Curation Impact." *International Journal of Digital Curation* 8 (2): 223–34. doi:10.2218/ijdc.v8i2.286.

Humanities Data Curation

Anderson, Deborah W., Alison Babeu, David Dubin, Katrina Fenlon, Julia Flanders, Jacob Jett, Melissa Levine, Trevor Munoz, Carole L. Palmer, and C.M. Sperberg-McQueen. *DH Curation Guide: a community resource guide to data curation in the digital humanities.* http://guide.dhcuration.org/.

Padilla, Thomas. 2016. "Humanities Data in the Library: Integrity, Form, Access." *DLib Magazine* 22 (3-4). doi:10.1045/march2016-padilla.

Scientific Data Curation

Akmon, Dharma, Ann Zimmerman, Morgan Daniels, and Margaret Hedstrom. 2011. "The Application of Archival Concepts to a Data-Intensive Environment: Working with Scientists to Understand Data Management and Preservation Needs." *Archival Science* 11 (3–4): 329–48. doi:10.1007/s10502-011-9151-4.

Baker, Karen S., and Lynn Yarmey. 2009. "Data Stewardship: Environmental Data Curation and a Web-of-Repositories." *International Journal of Digital Curation* 4 (2): 12–27. doi:10.2218/ijdc.v4i2.90.

Bechhofer, Sean, Iain Buchan, David De Roure, Paolo Missier, John Ainsworth, Jiten Bhagat, Philip Couch, et al. 2013. "Why Linked Data Is Not Enough for Scientists." *Future Generation Computer Systems* 29 (2): 599–611. doi:10.1016/j.future.2011.08.004.

Chao, Tiffany C., Melissa H. Cragin, and Carole L. Palmer. 2015. "Data Practices and Curation Vocabulary (DPCVocab): An Empirically Derived Framework of Scientific Data Practices and Curatorial Processes." *Journal of the Association for Information Science and Technology* 66 (3): 616–33. doi:10.1002/asi.23184.

Murillo, Angela P. 2014. "Data at Risk Initiative: Examining and Facilitating the Scientific Process in Relation to Endangered Data." *Data Science Journal* 12 (0): 207–19. doi:10.2481/dsj.12-048.

National Science Board. 2005. "Long-Lived Digital Data Collections Enabling Research and Education in the 21st Century." NSB-05-40. National Science Board.

Poole, Alex H. 2014. "How Has Your Science Data Grown? Digital Curation and the Human Factor: A Critical Literature Review." *Archival Science* 15 (2): 101–39. doi:10.1007/s10502-014-9236-y.

Roche, Dominique G., Loeske E. B. Kruuk, Robert Lanfear, and Sandra A. Binning. 2015. "Public Data Archiving in Ecology and Evolution: How Well Are We Doing?" *PLOS Biology* 13 (11): e1002295. doi:10.1371/journal.pbio.1002295.

Social Science Data Curation

Guide to Social Science Data Preparation and Archiving. 2012. 5th ed. Ann Arbor, Mich.: ICPSR. http://www.icpsr.umich.edu/files/ICPSR/access/dataprep.pdf.

Gutmann, Myron, Kevin Schürer, Darrell Donakowski, and Hilary Beedham. 2004. "The Selection, Appraisal, and Retention of Social Science Data." *Data Science Journal* 3: 209–21. doi:10.2481/dsj.3.209.

Vardigan, Mary, Pascal Heus, and Wendy Thomas. 2008. "Data Documentation Initiative: Toward a Standard for the Social Sciences." *International Journal of Digital Curation.* 3 (1): 107–13. doi:10.2218/ijdc.v3i1.45.

Researcher Assessments for Data Curation

Brandt, D. Scott, and Eugenia Kim. 2014. "Data Curation Profiles as a Means to Explore Managing, Sharing, Disseminating or Preserving Digital Outcomes." *International Journal of Performance Arts and Digital Media* 10 (1): 21–34. doi:10.1080/14794713.2014.912498.

Johnston, Lisa, Jacob Carlson, C.R.H. Vitale, Heidi Imker, Wendy Kozlowski, Robert Olendorf, and Claire Stewart. 2017a. "Results of the Fall 2016 Research Engagement Sessions through the Data Curation Network." https://docs.google.com/document/d/1ANiIdIChe6VPNloykMJFQEfAPJRGA8-zO-g8z7-XH7k/edit?usp=embed_facebook.

McLure, Merinda, Allison V. Level, Catherine L. Cranston, Beth Oehlert, and Mike Culbertson. 2014. "Data Curation: A Study of Researcher Practices and Needs." Portal: Libraries and the Academy 14 (2): 139–64. doi: 10.1353/pla.2014.0009.

Witt, Michael, Jacob Carlson, D. Scott Brandt, and Melissa H. Cragin. 2009. "Constructing Data Curation Profiles." *International Journal of Digital Curation* 4 (3): 93–103. doi:10.2218/ijdc.v4i3.117.

Data Curation Training and Education

Lee, Cal. 2009. "Matrix of Digital Curation Knowledge and Competencies (Overview)." *DigCCurr.* https://ils.unc.edu/digccurr/digccurr-matrix.html.

National Research Council. 2015. *Preparing the Workforce for Digital Curation.* https://www.nap.edu/catalog/18590/preparing-the-workforce-for-digital-curation.

Schmidt, Birgit and Kathleen Shearer. 2016. "Librarians' Competencies Profile for Research Data Management." *Joint Task Force on Librarians' Competencies in Support of EResearch and Scholarly Communication.* https://www.coar-repositories.org/files/Competencies-for-RDM_June-2016.pdf.

Data Repository Development and Requirements

Fallaw, Colleen, Elise Dunham, Elizabeth Wickes, Dena Strong, Ayla Stein, Qian Zhang, Kyle Rimkus, Bill Ingram, and Heidi J. Imker. 2016. "Overly Honest Data Repository Development." *The Code4Lib Journal* no. 34 (October). http://journal.code4lib.org/articles/11980.

Johnston, Lisa, ed. 2017. *Curating Research Data, Volume One: Practical Strategies for Your Digital Repository*. ACRL. http://www.alastore.ala.org/detail.aspx?ID=11960.

Leahey, Amber, Peter Webster, Claire Austin, Nancy Fong, Julie Friddell, Chuck Humphrey, Susan Brown, and Walter Stewart. 2015. "Research Data Repository Requirements and Features Review - RDC Standards & Interoperability Committee (SINC) Dataverse." https://dataverse.scholarsportal.info/dataset.xhtml?persistentId=hdl:10864/10892.

Data Copyright and Citation

Carroll, Michael W. 2015. "Sharing Research Data and Intellectual Property Law: A Primer." *PLOS Biology* 13 (8): e1002235. doi:10.1371/journal.pbio.1002235.

Lawrence, Bryan, Catherine Jones, Brian Matthews, Sam Pepler, and Sarah Callaghan. 2011. "Citation and Peer Review of Data: Moving Towards Formal Data Publication." *International Journal of Digital Curation* 6 (2): 4–37. doi:10.2218/ijdc.v6i2.205.

Additional Resources

Bailey, Jr., Charles W. 2017. "Research Data Curation Bibliography." January 24. http://digital-scholarship.org/rdcb/rdcb.htm.

Hudson-Vitale, Cynthia, Heidi Imker, Lisa R. Johnston, Jake Carlson, Wendy Kozlowski, Robert Olendorf, and Claire Stewart. Survey data for SPEC Kit 354: Data Curation (May 2017). https://github.com/1heidi/dcn_spec_kit_data.

Note: All URLs accessed April 3, 2017.